ULTI GUIDE TO E-COMMERCE GROWTH

7 Unexpected KPIs To Scale An E-commerce Shop To £10 Million Plus

ULTIMATE GUIDE TO SCALABLE E-COMMERCE
by IAN HAMMERSLEY and MARK HAMMERSLEY

ISBN-13: 978-1-64467-132-0

ULTIMATE GUIDE TO E-COMMERCE GROWTH

7 Unexpected KPIs To Scale An E-commerce Shop To £10 Million Plus

IAN HAMMERSLEY & MARK HAMMERSLEY

TABLE OF CONTENTS

Before we start, let me introduce to you the great companion video that goes alongside this book, which details some of the split tests we have run to improve some of the KPIs we are going to be talking about, so please head over to https://go.smartebusiness.co.uk/get-started-magento and sign up for the video and members' area for this book.

INTRODUCTION

Imagine, for a moment, your e-commerce website. Go ahead and picture it in your mind. Now think about why you and your team put it together the way you did. Maybe it has a clean look or trusted colours or an easy checkout process. You may have tweaked and re-tweaked it several times already and you're getting pretty good results.

But what if we told you that it's 100% likely that you're still missing out on at least 50% additional revenue?

Would that be enough to get your attention?

Would you want to know more?

What if we also told you that there are exact locations (like a blueprint or treasure map) on every e-commerce website that have been proven to be key performance areas, and most e-commerce sites are underperforming in these areas?

Now imagine that treasure map with piles of money just sitting there waiting for you to discover it. If you could have that kind of assurance—if you could have proof—that it's these same places on every website, every time, would you want to know where these places are?

Yes, well, it gets better.

Not only do these key places exist, but they are easy to get to, easy to understand, and learning how to make the necessary changes won't require any extra training, education or a huge investment in your time.

The only thing it's going to take is for you to have an understanding of where these key areas are and what they should look like to perform at their highest potential. Once you have this knowledge, which we are about to tell you, then you can go ahead and make these changes yourself (if you know how) or you can easily hire someone else to do it. The end result will be well worth the time it takes you to read this book and discover them.

Is it worth it to you?

If we promise to give you this information with no surprises, no hidden costs in the middle of this book and no long, drawn-out, boring stories to wade through, would you keep reading?

Good! We would too.

So wait. You're probably wondering who we are and why we think we know so much about e-commerce and making the most profit possible from your e-commerce website.

WHO THE HECK ARE THESE GUYS?

We are Mark and Ian Hammersley, brothers and directors of smartebusiness, a dedicated E-commerce agency based in Manchester. E-commerce is what we do. We specialise in the growth of e-commerce websites and have been scaling online businesses for the past 15 years.

It's what we are passionate about, and, quite frankly, it's what we and our team are extremely good at.

We are definitely self-confessed e-commerce geeks!

As promised, you're about to get about 15 years' worth of our 'Eureka!' moments packed into one extremely useful manual. It's going to allow you to get past what you *think* is wrong with your site and provide you with some solid, tested and accurate information that we've used with our e-commerce clients without fail.

You're about to learn how to spot the real problems. You're also going to learn to think the right way about your business, your product, and the value you bring to the marketplace!

We started smartebusiness together 15 years ago. We grew up listening to our parents talk shop around the dinner table, discussing how they could grow the family bakery business and all the trials and tribulations that went with it. We still remember every Easter celebrating each time we'd break the hot-cross-bun record, at a time when supermarkets were trying to destroy us. That's where we got our passion for business, and we try to run our clients' businesses as if they are our own.

Shoot back with us several years ago, and you'll see where our geekiness and knack for e-commerce sites began. Mark had recently moved to Auckland, New Zealand, but the agreement was that his job was to remain in the UK, working for the Manchester office. We were in a dilemma. How could we make it work when one of us was on the other side of the world? Everything seemed to be working against us: the time zone, the distance and the lack of market contact. It seemed like an uphill battle. But we knew that if we grew our clients' e-commerce revenues then the distance, time zone and everything else wouldn't matter. Clients want results, plain and simple. Give them results and you could live on Mars for all they care.

What did we have? We had access to the Google Analytics accounts of roughly 80 e-commerce stores and we knew that some sites were growing rapidly while others were stuck. So we closed ourselves off in our respective basements and got to work. We benchmarked every statistic we could get our hands on. After some work and a good deal of research, we started to recognise the key stats that mattered. Once these were pinpointed, we started making the changes that helped each commerce site get to the next level and the next and the next.

The result was that distance and time zone didn't matter because our clients became some of the fastest growing e-commerce sites in the UK.

And we want your e-commerce site to be part of that.

Are you ready?

Let's go!

WHAT DID WE SET OUT TO ACCOMPLISH?

Quite simply, we knew that if we grew our clients' e-commerce businesses then they would continue to invest more with us. We wanted our developers to be building e-commerce sites that did better. We didn't want to waste any time— our clients' or our own.

From the outside of the business, the problem was clear—stagnant e-commerce sites were asking us to help, but it just looked hopeless. Everything looked broken and needed fixing. There were a thousand things the client could try, but we needed to know what to do next that would make a difference. At the start, our clients didn't have the deep pockets of their Goliath competitors.

But for us personally, we wanted to have a great business to allow us to be a big part of each other's lives. We love working together, and the business we share allows us to talk every day. If we were to continue, we had to make this work. What's more, these were the most important years of our working lives, and we needed to achieve as much as we would if we were both living in the UK while making a life for our families.

THE WALL THAT HIT US IN THE FACE

They say that big breakthroughs only happen when you hit a wall. Well, SEO and Google was our wall. Google was massively changing SEO, which we used to drive a lot of free traffic to our clients. It was clear this method of growth was getting harder. We needed a new growth engine and fast. We had ignored the signs at first, but while on holiday, an employee phoned to tell us that our largest client's SEO rankings were acting weird. One day they went up, the next day they disappeared, then came back, then . . .

Google was changing their algorithm, and even when it settled down, we realised that we did not want our clients to rely on one source of revenue. Doing so could result in a single point of failure. We had to keep growing our clients' revenue, but without relying so heavily on Google as we had done in the past.

WHERE DO THE 96% GO?

No matter what type of product you sell, if you own a website, your number one goal is to convince visitors to put items in their basket, proceed to the checkout and complete the purchase.

Seems simple enough, right?

Of course, if you currently have an e-commerce website, you've probably realised there's more to making sales than just putting up a website and a shopping cart.

We've also learned that approximately 96% of customers who browse a site will leave without making a purchase, and that's being generous. Conversion rates of one or two percent are actually very common. This begs the following questions:

- ✓ Where are the 96% going?
- ✓ Who are the four percent?
- ✓ How did the four percent reach your website?
- ✓ What did the four percent do on your website?

DIGGING INTO THE 96%

We had all this data; we knew that some sites were doing very well, but what were they doing differently? Were there similarities between all the good websites, or were they all growing for different reasons? Even if we found something in the data, would it help?

The trouble was, we needed to look at the data from 80 sites and pull it all into Excel. To look at everything was going to take time, and we already had a full time job running a company, working weekends and looking after young families. When were we going to find a clear two weeks, or even longer, to do the work? Also, there was no guarantee anything was going to come out of this work. So nobody was rooting for us to do it—quite the opposite. We still needed to do all the SEO work, which was still our biggest breadwinner.

It came down to a tough decision. We could drop all my SEO clients and lose 75% of our marketing revenue to do the benchmarking study and hope something came out of it, or we could just continue as normal.

In my mind, SEO, at that particular time, was dead. Our minds were already made up. We dropped all our SEO clients. There was no turning back now—we needed to deliver something good!

However, after stressing out for months and months from gruelling research, we came up with nothing. We started losing hope; we just couldn't see why some clients were scaling and other clients were having stagnant growth at best. We just couldn't work it out. We had a crisis call where we were going to pull the plug on the research project. We'd spent over 300 hours poring through client statistics. We needed to have one last look at the high growth clients . . . then . . . we saw something magical. There was a consistent pattern.

After all of this painstaking work, we finally had our light bulb 'Eureka!' moment. It made all the difference in the success of our clients, and we're going to share this information now with you.

THE WAY FORWARD

The benchmarking study showed me that the successful, rapidly growing websites all had the same attributes that consistently underlined their growth. Seven key characteristics seemed to totally dominate a site's success. These are listed below, and we dive into each one in more depth later on.

1. Add-to-basket rate.
2. Website speed and capacity.
3. Lifetime customer value.
4. Growth of six-month customer recruitment year on year.
5. Average order value robustness.

6. Traffic growth.

7. Basket-to-order rate.

THE INGREDIENTS THAT ALLOWED ONE OF OUR CLIENTS TO GROW REVENUE BY 23 TIMES

When we first found these KPIs from the benchmarking study, we thought we were going to sound like one of those self-help books. You know, like *Just Do These Seven Things and You Will Become a Billionaire*. However, we realised we had not stumbled upon the seven things to do but rather the seven ingredients needed for e-commerce growth. It's like baking a cake. In order to make one, you need to know all of the ingredients, but you also need to know how to combine them and in which order to combine them.

The seven KPIs were the ingredients. They were the WHAT but not the HOW. Determining how to use the KPIs comes from all the experience we have had growing e-commerce revenue.

This is not a quick fix. Using the KPIs and achieving success with them requires knowing how to apply them, when to apply them and where. You have to put in the work in order for the KPIs to succeed.

These KPIs have allowed us to grow the revenue of brooktaverner.co.uk by over 23 times, compared to the monthly revenue when we first took them on as a client. The KPIs serve as a constant indication of the growth potential. They allow you to look at the metrics and instantly know where the growth potential is. These KPIs take away the guess work and remove emotion from the decisions of what to do. They tell you what, why and when to invest in your e-commerce store. In addition, the KPIs show when investing in certain areas of your site will give you no revenue gain whatsoever. Whenever growth slowed, you could be sure that one of these KPIs had reduced.

HOW OUR CUSTOMERS REALISED THE DIFFERENCE BETWEEN MARGIN ERODING BIG SALES AND SUSTAINABLE GROWTH

We weren't convinced these KPIs would apply to all e-commerce sites. Would they work on business to business (B2B) sites as well as they worked on websites with high-priced items?

To find out, we tested a large selection of B2B sites, and oddly, these metrics seemed almost more important to B2B sites due to their reliance on repeat business. With sites that sold high-ticket items, often there was a one-off sale and little repeat; however, this just made some of the KPIs less important. As long as these KPIs didn't reduce while the other metrics increased then sustainable growth followed.

ONE CLIENT BROKE A THREE YEAR FLAT SALES RUN WITH THESE METRICS

What about those clients who had tried everything to boost their revenue? Well, we believe a lot of marketing moves one KPI but reduces another. For example, you might increase your add-to-basket rate but this might reduce your six-month-recruitment rate. Thus, if you try to improve without monitoring all these KPIs, you can end up frustrated because you cannot see the whole picture—it's like trying to fill a bucket with a hole in it.

One client wanted to hit growth hard and kept upping their AdWords budgets. Their sales looked great but the KPIs told us that these new customers didn't buy again as quickly as the historical customers had done. Therefore, we could forecast this was going to cripple their future lifetime customer value and thus sales. But the client didn't know this and so kept increasing the AdWords budget.

When we came on board we could pinpoint that SOME of the extra traffic was adding good customers. We also helped determine which customers they didn't want. Thus, they were able to recruit the right type of customers, increase their ad spend and move back into growth for the first time in three years.

THE PLAN

Knowing what to track and why was great, but if you don't make these KPIs easy to track and monitor, then it's just a lot of theory. So we created a series of reporting measurements to track these KPIs on all the e-commerce sites we were growing—because we know that what gets measured gets managed. A lot of these metrics were not available in Google Analytics, so we had to create a tracking tool called ScentTrail to monitor them. Then we worked out for each client their weak points and target KPIs. We then created a list of implementations that had helped other clients improve each KPI. We ran a 'plan, do, check, act' methodology to uncover what implementations moved the needles in the right direction.

THE RESULT

Once we had these metrics, the work was only half done. We needed to know how to improve all these KPIs, and that just came down to experience. By focusing on these numbers every day, getting the whole team to understand the true purpose of an e-commerce site and talking to the clients in the new language meant we all achieved growth much faster. Clients like Brook Taverner grew into a big player in the menswear market, generating 23 times the monthly revenue that they did when we first took them on. GSF Car Parts took their online business from scratch to seven figures in their first year and continue to experience yearly double-digit growth. We've helped four e-commerce business owners grow and sell their business for high multimillion pound figures. Our team has won awards for our work as voted by our clients. We have also helped FTSE-listed companies increase their EBIT number and achieve their targets, such is the success of these key metrics.

But a lot of the things we found fly in the face of a lot of the advice we read online about how to grow. A lot of what we suggest will put us in 'e-commerce jail' and many online experts will find our clients' e-commerce stores annoyingly successful!

We don't do a lot of stuff that people tell us we should do.

They tell us to put a quick view on the category pages.

We refuse.

They tell us to use single product Adgroups in Google Shopping.

We don't.

They tell us we should never discount.

We fail.

They tell us to split AdWords campaigns by device.

We resist.

They tell us to remarket to everyone.

We avoid.

They tell us we need the latest extension on our sites.

We ignore them.

They tell us we should be getting into 'native' advertising.

We yawn.

They tell us we should have fancy dropdowns.

We tune out.

Why?

Because we don't care what the *latest* trend is. We are always testing, testing, testing. Everything has to prove itself, and often what these 'experts' recommend is just baloney.

It's baloney because what works for one site does not always work for another.

You cannot play football in flippers or snooker with a table tennis bat.

At least, not very well.

The wrong technique on the wrong site is bad.

THE MAGIC BULLET

To all our problems, we want to take a pill and wake up the next morning fixed.

'Too poor? Take this pill and wake up rich!'

It's silly; it's snake oil, yet people still look for it. With our e-commerce sites, there is no magic bullet.

You are not going to make one change and become a billionaire. Anyone that tells you different is a liar.

Even seemingly overnight successes are built on solid foundations. Some retailer might say 'We implemented x, and our sales doubled.' This is possible only because of prior work.

For example, one client implemented an Amazon Prime-style free delivery offer.

The conversion rate of existing customers doubled.

But . . .

This was only possible because the existing customers loved the products and the store. The existing customers were looking for an excuse to buy more.

Years of preparation had gone into that magic bullet moment.

Another client doubled their Google Shopping campaigns by changing their AdWords setup. Yes, we doubled sales, but months of offer testing and conversion rate optimisation had gone into that trigger moment.

Magic bullet moments happen. Watershed events where the potential in your brand is released.

However, there is no tipping point without preparation.

THE KEY PERFORMANCE INDICATORS (KPIS)

Wait . . . what is a key performance indicator?

A key performance indicator is pretty much just what you'd think it would be. It is a measurable value used to indicate how effective a business is at achieving its objectives. In our case, the final objective is a completed sale, but there are KPIs along the way that we can use to track and evaluate performance, so we can really dial in and discover where the problem areas might be and ultimately increase revenue.

These KPIs are important to how your site operates. Remember, when you're small you can't simply copy what a larger site is doing and hope it works. A massive brand is going to be more successful than an unknown online store. Copying their website isn't going to help your site perform better. For this, you need your KPIs in place.

WHERE TO START

On average:
- ✓ 11% of visitors will add a product to their basket.
- ✓ Of that 11%, 55% will proceed to checkout.
- ✓ Of that 55%, 84% will place an order.

To determine how your website is doing, first benchmark yourself against these three statistics. If you're falling behind in one of these, then this will dictate where you need to spend your time and money. For instance, if you only have five percent of your visitors placing items in their cart, then this is where your energy and time needs to be. You'll need to answer the question, "Why aren't visitors adding items to their cart?"

Or you might find that your add-to-basket percentage is high but very few people are proceeding to checkout: the dreaded abandoned cart syndrome!

Most e-commerce platforms offer a variety of strong merchandising techniques to help with these situations. In the following chapters, we'll discuss the three key performance indicators, or KPIs, and a few of the techniques to help you increase the percentage of these three KPIs.

GET YOUR E-COMMERCE SITE TO THE GYM

Think of these KPIs as your website's fitness level. When Mark first started going to the gym, even a small workout left him exhausted.

He dreaded it. He could not figure out how some people could spend hours on those machines and then do a full day's work.

But now he can go to the gym, do a workout and not have to lie down afterwards.

This is an improvement.

Of course, now he can move onto other things, do more weights, do more cardio. Those activities are available to him.

So how fit is your website? Imagine marketing spend as exercise for your website.

How much 'spend' can it cope with before it needs to lie down?

For a human, fitness can be measured by KPIs such as VO2 max and speed. For a website, fitness is measured by add-to-basket rate, basket-to-order rate and the other KPIs we will introduce you to in this book.

If your website is not fit, it's never going to compete in a marathon against the top competition. However, your revenue goals probably means it needs to.

We were looking at two websites yesterday, both sites owned by the same client; one targets high end and the other the value market. The high-end website, we have got fit: the add to basket is now hitting 9% having moved from 5%, and it's hitting its target nicely and scaling ad spend. But the value website, even though add to basket has moved from 3% to 6%, still needs work. It's not fit enough to scale. Luckily, there is still a lot of obvious stuff to fix, namely:

- The mobile site has the menu burger and the basket icons in the wrong places, meaning people can't find them.
- The basket page is messy.
- There is little social proof on the website.
- The reviews are good but hidden away.

We feel like personal trainers, training a client to compete in a marathon. These KPIs are your website's fitness level—if they are low they are never going to cope with the adspend you need to hit your revenue goals.

ADD-TO-
BASKET RATE

This is the unique add to baskets per session divided by the sessions. It all started here, and we just kept coming back to this metric. All the sites were doing poorly where this KPI was concerned. If the add-to-basket rate was low, then it didn't matter about the checkout. It became our go-to metric for new sites, the place we would work on first. We would split test and implement to move this metric up. Sometimes a split test would move the revenue per visitor up but lower the add-to-basket metric, so we iterated until both metrics went up as this gave us more users to improve later in the funnel. This is easily measured in Google Analytics via Google Analytics Events or via tagging for Google Analytics Enhanced E-commerce.

BOING . . . BOING!

Out of all the individuals landing on your website, some of them are going to bounce off. This can occur from any page on your site. Some may bounce off the home page, others may get to a category page or product page before making their exit. Some even put items in their basket and proceed to the checkout page before they decide to abandon ship. And then there's the four percent who make it through checkout and place an order.

A good place to start improving your add-to-basket rate is to look at your bounce rate across content types. For example, how do product pages or category pages perform as a whole? By understanding this, you can easily monitor improvements made to the product templates.

Key performance indicator (KPI) number one is what we call the add-to-basket percentage, and it is definitely the most critical one. If no one is adding anything to their basket in the first place, there's definitely a problem.

According to the statistics we work with, 11% of visitors to your website should add something to their basket.

So what if you're not at that percentage? There's a good chance you may not be; that's why you are reading this book!

We're going to help you figure out why.

When we first consult with our clients, the majority of them think they have a problem with the checkout process itself. Upon inspection of their site, however, we often find out that their checkout is just fine. What they are really struggling with is getting visitors to put items in their basket.

ADD-TO-BASKET PERCENTAGE

The first thing you need to think about when trying to get visitors to put your product in their basket is the type of buyers you're working with. For example, by analysing the buyer types, it allowed us to see why on one high-growth site a marketing message reduced conversion and on another high-growth site it massively increased it. How so?!! It was the same message . . .

It was all down to these four buyer types and how you've got to understand who yours are. By looking at the different types of buyers, we were able to determine why one site worked while another didn't, even when the same marketing message was used. Consider the following chart:

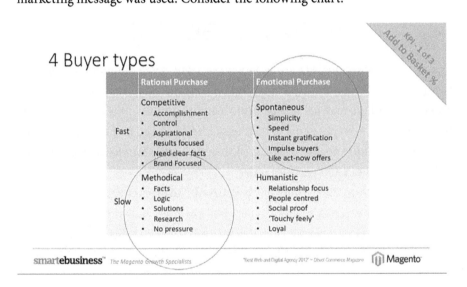

There are four types of buyers:
- ✓ Competitive.
- ✓ Spontaneous.
- ✓ Methodical.
- ✓ Humanistic.

THE COMPETITIVE TYPE

Think James Bond.

James Bond mentions his tailor with fondness a few times during the Bond movies.

I am talking about the James Bond of old, not the modern Bond who doesn't give a damn how his vodka martini is served.

The James Bond we grew up with was a connoisseur of attire, wine and history. He cared about the finer things in life.

When we are selling to the discerning buyer, we need to build that loyalty in our customers, and they will never leave.

The James Bond buyer can be classed as the competitive buyer type.

This buyer type wants the best, buys quickly and is not a sales shopper as they are less sensitive to price.

So how did Mr Bond's tailor generate the loyalty to bring him back time and time again?

Here's how we would have done it.

We would have made sure that our shop was an authority in men's tailoring. This can be done by:

- Sponsoring events that already have the authority I am seeking to borrow.
- Working with clients who have authority and giving them good stories to tell about their experience. I want them to talk about their tailor down at the country club.
- Making my clients perceive that it's exclusive by making them apply for a fitting. To generate discussions about this 'oh, it's very hard to get an appointment at X tailor, he is very in demand.' This is like catnip to the competitive buyer
- Having a store on Savile Row 'where everyone knows the best tailors are.'

Next, I would have to make the shop experience bespoke, no fuss and flawless.

The competitive buyer hates incompetence. They want you to notice the finer detail without it being pointed out.

They know how a suit should hang, what stitching should be done where, but they never want to have to tell you this; they expect you to know and to get it done.

When they go in for a suit fitting, it should feel like a seamless process from start to finish. Great services look easy because so much planning and time has gone into the preparation.

Then we come to delivery.

We would know that our client travels a lot, and we would want to make it easy for the client to pick up the suit.

We would need to tailor our delivery options to suit the client, even liaising with our client's secretary to have the suit delivered without the client having to think about it.

If something went wrong with the delivery, we would need to forget about the profitability of that one order and make sure that the suit was delivered on time.

The thought would be on the service even when delivery might be impossible.

'Impossible delivery' builds some great customer stories, which we want our authority clients to spread.

After all, this the product needs to perform, and if it doesn't, we need to take care of it, no questions asked.

At the end of the day, we are not providing a suit for Mr Bond.

Instead, we are providing a method for Mr Bond to show that he is a man not to be trifled with.

Today Mr Bond's team would order replacement garments from an online store.

He needs a new shirt; the site would be personalised to his sizing information, orders would be easy and his orders would be reviewed personally by his tailor in case a team member made a mistake.

Just because the world has moved online does not mean that we must ignore the top competitive buyers.

Now that we are online, there is a greater opportunity to extend the flawless experience for the competitive buyer.

THE METHODICAL TYPE

We love watching old *Columbo* murder mysteries. He is like the atypical hero: scruffy, appearing disorganised but probably the greatest detective in the world.

He lulls the murderer into a false sense of security. The murderer thinks the police department has sent an idiot to solve the crime.

But he keeps asking questions.

'Just one more thing . . .'

Often this comes after a long conversation when his suspect is already annoyed. The questions keep coming. It's the detail in the answers that he analyses. Over and over until the murderer slips up.

Columbo's manner is humble, apologetic and bumbling but incredibly effective. We all have Columbo customers visiting our stores every day. They are the methodical buyer type.

They spend a long time buying. They need answers to a lot of questions. They scroll the full page. They read the reviews onsite and offsite.

And just when you think you have done enough, they abandon your website. They abandon because we are not the murderer.

The murderer is the solution to their mystery, which is 'where can I buy the best *xyz*?' They find the murderer somewhere else, somewhere that provides better answers, more details and more evidence. But how many Columbo-buyer types are there in our traffic and why should we care?

Well, usually a lot. On most stores, this is the biggest of the four buyer types and can make up over 50% of potential customers.

You need to start creating more evidence, on your site, for Columbo to stumble upon.

THE SPONTANEOUS TYPE

I once watched a documentary about Michael Jackson and part of it showed him going shopping in a home décor shop in Las Vegas. It was like he was picking out sweets even though these were $89,000 pieces of furniture. "I like those, lets order those . . . and these . . . and these, this table and these."

The spontaneous buyer buys very quickly and does so on impulse with very little fact checking. Whilst we will always have some spontaneous buyers coming to our stores, most of them will show up at sale times. Normal buyers will be transformed into spontaneous buyers during promotions like Black Friday, Cyber Monday, Boxing Day Sales, etc.

Spontaneous buyers like to have things right in front of them. They are shopping for fun, and they don't like to search or work to find something to buy. During sale times, we must create a home page that suggests what they should buy and show them a good quick reason for doing to.

THE HUMANISTIC TYPE

The humanistic buyer is driven by emotion and does not like to buy from a brand until they feel a connection with the store. This buyer type is triggered more when they are making a purchase of something for their home and family. They tend to take more time over the purchase and really dive into the reviews and the ethos behind the company.

IS IT RATIONAL OR EMOTIONAL?

These four types of buyers also fall into one of two purchasing camps: they either make rational or emotional purchases.

THE RATIONAL PURCHASE

A rational purchase describes a product that is necessary and often purchased only when it is going to solve a fundamental, immediate problem. A car battery, for instance, is a rational, distressed purchase. If you sent an email to customers offering 80% off a car battery or even a buy-one-get-one-free car battery deal, they aren't likely to have any interest in your offer unless they absolutely need a car battery right now. This type of purchase offers a small window of opportunity for a sale. You probably have four to six hours to get the sale so the buying window is incredibly small.

THE EMOTIONAL PURCHASE

An emotional purchase, on the other hand, is something a buyer might want, but doesn't necessarily need, like a set of decorative cushions, a handbag or other products that have aesthetic value. Fashion mainly falls into this camp, though a dinner suit for a black tie event tomorrow night would be considered more rational/problem solving. Customers may respond better to a discount of 40% or free shipping with an item like this because it is an impulsive, spontaneous purchase. For emotional purchases, the buying window is much longer. In some cases where it's a high average order value and very emotional, it can be several months.

Because these two types of purchases are so different from each other and appeal to different types of buyers, you'll need to use a different strategy to encourage each type of buyer to put your product in the basket. For the more rational purchase, you'll want to appeal to the urgency and need of the item. In this instance, a **quick delivery time, adverts with text like 'huge range' and an onsite countdown timer** would be much more likely to result in a completed transaction than a discount offer alone.

If the product is an emotional purchase, like the decorative cushions, using larger images showing the item nicely displayed in a beautiful home or discounts that are 'ending soon' are more likely to appeal to the buyer. Remember, they don't *need* the cushions. No one *needs* cushions. They aren't going to solve some fundamental problem in anyone's life, but if your web visitor likes them and they are displayed and presented properly, you're likely to get a sale. That's the beauty of the emotional purchase.

IDENTIFY YOUR BUYER

The first thing you need to think about when addressing the add-to-basket KPI is whether you are selling a rational, problem-solving product or an emotional one.

THE MARKET SQUARE ANALOGY—WHAT VALUE DO YOU PROVIDE?

In addition to determining what type of buyer you're appealing to and what kind of product you're selling, you'll also need to think about your unique **value proposition**. When talking to our clients about value proposition, we always encourage them to think about their business as if it were a brick-and-mortar building in a market square. Why? Because in reality, your online competition is going to be similar to that of the competition you would experience in a market square.

Imagine your customer walks into a market square—let's pretend your business is located all the way at the back end. In order to get to your store, the customer has to literally walk past other businesses selling the exact same items you are. These businesses may have discounts and special offers like free delivery, a no-quibble return policy, a selection of merchandise that's been discounted 30 or 40% off, or buy-one-get-one-free offers. If your market stall was just sitting there at the back, doing nothing to entice customers to pass these other businesses and come to you, they aren't going to come. You have to get out there and increase your value proposition in order to sell your product. You need to build tangible proof that your business is the best option for what the customer wants. Customers will walk past all the other businesses if they believe in your service and products.

Think about a market square

- Who your **real online competitors** are
- What call to actions and **offers?**
- **Social media** Strategy
- **What emails are they sending**, how many?
- How do they **collect email** addresses?
- How do they emphasise their **value proposition?**
- What their **prices** are like compared to yours?
- What is their **product photography** like compared to you?
- How are their **product descriptions** better or worse than yours?
- Are their **delivery options** more compelling than yours?

KPI - 1 of 3
Add to Basket %

smart**ebusiness**™ *The Magento Growth Specialists*   "Best Web and Digital Agency 2012" – *Direct Commerce Magazine*    Magento

There has to be a match between the look of your website and your value proposition in order for you to continue to scale your business. Your e-commerce site could be aesthetically perfect and easy to use and have all the bells and whistles, but your value proposition will always be the key to your success or failure.

On the other hand, a website can be plain and poorly put together, but if the value proposition is right and the product is something customers really want, this poor website will outperform an amazing-looking site every time. Now, certainly we can increase sales for the poorly put together site just by giving our client a sleek-looking website that really matches their excellent value proposition—then they will really take off.

What if you aren't feeling one hundred percent confident about your value proposition? How do you increase it?

Glad you asked . . . that's next.

But before we get to that, let us tell you a little story about cloning.

Monhish Pabrai is one of my favourite investors; apart from having an amazing track record at investing, he rose to fame as one of the first people to buy a charity lunch with Warren Buffet for $650,000 USD.

He said the lunch was worth every penny.

One of Monhish's favourite concepts is cloning, and he tells a good story about two petrol station owners to illustrate why some businesses fail.

Two petrol stations set up across the road from each other. Owner A starts filling the gas manually and cleaning the cars' windows. The owner B across the road sees this and says to his assistant, 'There's no point manually filling the gas and doing the windows as he can't do this for every car—people will get annoyed when they return, and they have to fill their car themselves. I am not doing that.'

And so it goes; he even tells owner A how stupid he is.

Over time, owner A's business starts to take off and more people choose to use his petrol station than owner B's.

But owner B does nothing.

Even though owner B knows exactly what is making the other petrol station busier over time, he still does not clone owner A.

Why?

Because he has invested and publicly stated his opinion that manually filling some cars is a waste of time.

He will desperately try to find some *other* way of growing his business so he doesn't have to admit being wrong. Also, he certainly doesn't want owner A to see him admitting defeat.

We have seen this a lot with some e-commerce clients who have been going a long time and a young new business comes into their market and starts cleaning up.

It's clear what the new business is doing; we reverse engineer the upstart and tell our client 'here's the plan.'

But they won't do it.

They want something different, something no-one else has ever done. They want the world to think they are a genius.

But unfortunately, most of us are average (duh), and so to have a fighting chance, we need to shamelessly clone what's working for others and then improve it.

Don't be too proud to make a lot of profit.

Stop trying to recreate the wheel.

Two quotes to sum this up.

Steve Jobs: 'We have always been shameless about stealing great ideas.'

Picasso: 'Good artists copy, great artists steal.'

Now you don't want to blindly copy your competition and be exactly the same as everyone else. However, if one customer is totally cleaning up, then at least do what they are doing and then improve it!

MERCHANDISING YOUR PRODUCT PAGES AND CATEGORY PAGES

Increasing your value proposition is most often linked to your product pages. Google Shopping has changed in recent years. Now, when customers click on products listed on the Google Shopping search page, they are taken straight to the product page of your site. Customers no longer have to navigate through your home page or visit a category page prior to reaching the product they are looking to buy. Google Shopping is a big, emerging traffic builder and most of the traffic relies on your product pages as the first impression of your site.

When the Google switch first occurred, we immediately noticed a high bounce rate on our clients' product pages. Some were over 75%, which is huge for an e-commerce site. The typical bounce rate for a product page should be less than 60%. This told us that potential customers were landing on the product page, but instead of buying, they were clicking back into their browser or hitting the Back button to return to Google and continue their product search. Product pages are now the new landing pages. The old days of visitors landing on home page > category page > product page are long over.

What we discovered is that when a product page displays only one product, it may be close but not the exact product your customer is looking for. If there are no other options for the customer to consider, they immediately exit the page and attempt to find a different product that fits their needs.

With one of our clients, a big-name cookware website, we found that by merchandising each product page and offering similar yet different alternatives on the same page, we were able to reduce the bounce rate by 35% and increase the add-to-basket KPI substantially.

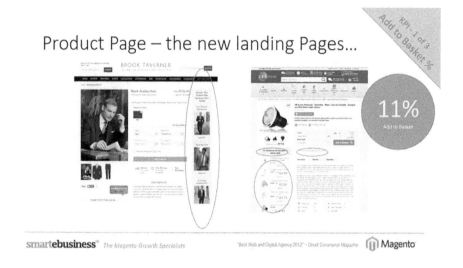

YOUR PRODUCT PAGE HAS THE POWER OF A LANDING PAGE

This really showed us how important individual product pages actually are. They have become the new landing pages of your website and work much harder than they used to. This means your product pages, if developed properly, have much more power than previously.

Category pages may not be as important when it comes to Google Shopping clicks, but they should not be ignored either. On average, we found that category pages should not be bouncing more than 55% . With these pages, there are several different methods that can be used to quickly pull a customer in and help him or her click on a product. Ease of navigation is another big booster for the add-to-basket rate.

Some methods include:

- ✓ Placing bestsellers at the top.
- ✓ Using the Image Attribute System.
- ✓ Spontaneous offers at the top.
- ✓ User reviews.

Category Page

- Bestsellers at the top
- New in splashes
- Spontaneous offers at the top
- Show reviews
- Bring in the reassurances

smart**e**business™ *The Magento Growth Specialists*   "Best Web and Digital Agency 2012" - *Direct Commerce Magazine*   🔷 Magento

FIRST IMPRESSIONS COUNT

Have you heard of the psychological effect of anchoring? This bias affects us all.

Inside our heads, we think we are rational human beings making sane judgements based on sensible thinking.

However, we are swayed by everything we see and hear, especially the most recent.

In *Thinking Fast and Slow*, Daniel Kahneman ran an experiment with his partner Amos where they had a Wheel of Fortune pre-set to only stop at 10 and 65. After spinning the wheel people were asked, 'What is your best guess of the percentage of African nations in the UN?'

Those people who saw 10 and 65 had average estimates of 25% and 45% respectively.

Other experiments have gone on to show that even when we know we are being shown a high anchor, we still are affected by it.

This is why:

- Those market stall pitches start with a high number. 'I would normally charge you £560 for this set of plastic vegetable chopping gizmos, but I am not going to even charge you £250; instead . . .'
- Stores mark up to mark down. So they can show a *was high* anchoring price.

- Jewellery is expensive—even though diamonds are practically worthless second hand, a high retail price triggers the 'expensive is good.'
- The last experience of someone's holiday has a huge impact on the review they give. So savvy hoteliers make the checkout and last night an amazing experience.

Even though we know this is going on, we are not immune.

So we e-commerce owners must be careful what we show the visitor before they reach the website. Therefore, bidding on brand on Google AdWords is important—as we can control the message they see before they visit the site. The organic listing often lacks punch and anchoring.

The first image they see on landing is also critical to their subsequent experience. That image will anchor their whole experience on the site. Split testing landing page images is one of the most rewarding activities you can do.

The first review they see on a Google Search for 'Brand Name Review' will anchor the following reviews.

The products on the top line of the category will anchor the experience of the other products. Try putting one expensive product in the top line of each category to see what happens to your average order value.

If you do offer coupons, try making the before price bigger and the after price smaller in font sizes. How does this affect conversion?

DOES THE SITE APPEAR EASY TO USE?

You may be aware of the famous experiment by Daniel Simons where he asks people to watch a video and count how many times a ball is thrown.

After watching the video, people are asked if they 'saw the gorilla.'

In the video, a person in a gorilla suits walks onto the screen and beats their chest and then exits. It's obvious, but 50% of people taking the experiment missed it.

Daniel Simons calls this attentional blindness.

This blindness comes from the way our eyes are built and minds wired. The high-resolution parts of the eye are small and use a lot of energy to use, thus we can only focus on a small amount of an image at any one time. We believe we are seeing the whole picture as the subconscious fills in the rest of the image with what 'it expects to be there.'

This is so powerful that, in conversion rate optimization, perceived ease of use is pretty much aligned with actual ease of use.

That's quite a powerful statement, if you think about it.

It means that if your website looks easy to use, then people will find it easy to use. But if it looks hard to use, then people will find it hard to use, even if it isn't.

People focus on what they believe is the truth and look for corroboration that aligns with that. It's too hard for the brain to constantly change its opinion, especially for something like buying from an e-commerce site where they are in 'leisure mode.'

Looking at attention blindness first in relation to an e-commerce site, people only focus on a small part of the screen, and optimising the parts they focus on will have a huge impact on revenue per visitor.

Optimising the parts of the site they don't focus on is a waste of time.

We can find out which parts of the home page, product page, category pages, basket pages and checkout pages people look at using a heat map tool. The hot spots are the places where you want to focus your split test work. They are the small parts of the site that are focused on and will disproportionately affect the user's impression of the store.

Also, take a step back and ask if your website looks easy to use? Are the Add to Basket buttons clear in a different colour and big and obvious? Ditto with the Proceed to Checkout buttons. Are there elements you can remove to clear clutter to allow more white space to highlight what the user should do?

Remember, if they think the site is easy to use, it will be easy to use.

A five-year-old should be able to figure out what to do.

When its our e-commerce site, we look at it with different eyes as our e-commerce site is our livelihood—it's a major focus in our lives. Thus, we can see a lot more on the site than the normal person because our focus is much higher. This extra focus makes us think we can add more elements, multiple home page offers, and still get more revenue. But the customer has other things in their life that they must focus more on; hence they can only give our site a narrow focus.

We must treat that narrow focus with care and understand that if we ask for too much focus energy from a visitor, they will bounce.

BEST SELLERS AT THE TOP AND IMAGE ATTRIBUTES

Most e-commerce platforms offer automated image attributes and plugins that let you arrange your products according to algorithms that will be most conducive to making a sale. You definitely don't have to do the work yourself, manually adding the tags to new items or best sellers. Site extensions will do this for you, so take advantage of that.

SORT YOUR HOMEPAGE TRAFFIC INTO BUCKETS

Recently, we read *Ask* by Ryan Levesque. It's one of those books that we need to pick back up and have another look at. In a nutshell, he gets in front of a large river of buying traffic and asks them what they want.

He then splits the majority of this into (up to five) buckets.

Then he creates a landing page that asks people which bucket they are in and sends them to a sales page crafted exactly for that bucket.

He knows that 80% of the traffic will fall into one of these five buckets and thus will get their own carefully crafted sales letter or offer.

Super simple and super effective.

Yet very few people do it.

Let's look at an example of how this might work on your homepage.

Take someone selling golfing equipment. Surveying the traffic in the golfing niche might lead you to the following buckets:

- First time golfers looking for their first golf clubs.
- Parents looking to buy clubs for their children.
- Intermediate golfers looking to move to the next level.
- Advanced golfers looking for the latest hot product.
- Everyone else.

Once we have the buckets, we can craft a simple home page survey to understand which person we are dealing with, i.e. 'Get Started With Our Five-Second Survey.'

Then we can lead, for example, the parents to a landing page talking about how to choose the right set of golf clubs for their child, covering what size to buy based on the child's height, etc. This will convert that buyer much more than a generic home page trying to convert all five buckets.

This approach makes so much sense.

But hardly anyone uses it.

Why?

Because we *think* we know the buyer. We *think* that we know exactly what should go on the homepage and that we can't afford to miss anyone.

It's the fear of not appealing to all traffic that stops us doing this approach.

You hear it across all small businesses when you ask, 'Who is your customer?' And they answer, 'Well, men and women 18 years to 65.'

Basically, their target market is human beings who have a bit of money.

We need to stop selling to everyone and do a good job of selling to the 20% of buyer categories that make up 80% of the traffic.

It's a good book; have a read, and then use your homepage to shift people into the five main buckets that your buyers represent.

SHOW YOUR REVIEWS

Reviews are going to build trust in your potential customer. Many shoppers actually won't buy from websites that don't post reviews because they rely heavily on the opinions and referral of others. Also, make sure your reviews are from a third party like Feefo or Trustpilot so that they are more believable and you get the review stars on your Google AdWords adverts.

And remember, you are supposed to be thinking of your e-commerce site just like a regular shop that someone could walk into. You wouldn't have just one item in the display window, would you? That would be ineffective. So, it's important to merchandise your product pages just the same way you'd move items around in a physical store, bringing best sellers to the front, displaying accessories with the items they match and placing new merchandise in a prominent place.

IMPROVE YOUR PRODUCT COPY AND OFFERS

If your products sell themselves via great imagery but then when the buyers dig into the detail the product copy looks like it was written by the accounts team, then you are going to lose the sale.

With product copy, we are trying to influence the visitor into buying the product. In terms of influence, you can find no better than Professor Robert Cialdini who literally wrote the book on influence.

We have been studying Cialdini for years, and here is our top checklist on how to bring some Cialdini magic to your product copy and store. We use this list when we are trying to increase the conversion rate of an e-commerce store by focusing on the buyer journey.

1. Are we using the law of reciprocity? What small item can we use to trigger this law? Can we use free samples or give something unexpected away with the first order?

2. The reason why. Are we giving them a reason why they should do what we want? Even *because* and repeating the obvious is better than nothing. Don't just have an offer, have a reason why there is an offer.

3. Law of comparison. If you show something hot first, the next thing will be considered much colder than it is; for example, show expensive items first to make items appear better value. Estate agents show crappy houses first. For example, can you have one expensive item in the category? How does this affect average order value (AOV)?

4. Can we trigger the 'expensive equals good' rule and then discount to make them want a bargain? (Does not work with commoditised products, only own brand.)

5. If we offer something much more expensive and they reject it, then we offer what we want them to accept, they will more likely accept. For example, offer three-year support plan then one-year support plan.

6. Consistency. Can we get the person to make a small step in the area we want? Later, changing direction will be harder for them: for example, getting them to fill out a survey telling us what they like about our brand. Mental commitment subconsciously.

7. Like previous point. During the sales process, we can ask them questions

like, 'Why are you considering purchasing from us?' They will create a rational answer and want to be consistent with it. Or even if the sale takes a while to close, ask, 'Can you tell me why you have chosen to do business with us?'

8.   Can we get them to write down their consistency statement and get them to share it publicly? Once public, they will change their image of themselves to be consistent with the statement even more. Could be part of a competition.

9.   Low ball offer. Make an offer that's likely to be accepted to make the person convince themselves that they are now a customer of the store. Once they have bought something, even something tiny, they will be much more likely to make a bigger purchase.

10. Social proof. If we can show that others are doing what we desire the visitor to do, then they will follow suit. People look to others to see what to do.

11. Social proof heightened. People will much more likely copy behaviour of people like themselves. Even similar names, living in similar addresses, doing the same jobs, etc.

12. When the buyer is in a moment of uncertainty, we can employ opera claqueurs, i.e. the first people that get the crowd going. We have all seen those market stall people use fake buyers to start a buying frenzy at the end of their pitch.

13. Can we show that we dress like the target audience and share similar values to them? Political views. Hobbies.

14. Can we associate ourselves even loosely with something cool going on? For example, during the moon landings, everything sold featured the space race. Or in Olympic years, everything focuses on this.

15. Click-whirr effect of authority figures. Uniform. Titles. Name badges. Backstage passes. Can we add elements of this to increase the sale?

16. If we offer them something that is against our interest that builds trust early on, for example, don't buy this, buy our cheaper one if *xyz*. Or show them some bad reviews on our site for some products so that they believe the good reviews.

17. Double scarcity. People who were told beef is going to be in short supply doubled their orders. But people told beef supply is going to be in short supply and told this information comes from an exclusive source bought

a huge amount more. So how can we create scarcity on our stores and make customers believe that they are getting inside information about the scarcity—premium buyers' clubs etc.?

18. Can we trigger the scarcity trigger by getting all potential buyers to show up at once onto one product and show how many people are looking at that item? Or even get them to reserve a buying spot, where they get 10 minutes to decide on the product before the chance is offered to someone else.

MANAGE BY EXCEPTION

A few years ago, we began to look at the product pages and category pages that had the highest bounce rates in more detail because we wanted to work on our worst performers to bring their sales up. To do this, we tagged them properly and used Google Analytics, so we could see, in detail, the worst product pages and worst category pages.

Why would we work from the poorest performers?

Attempting to analyse hundreds or even thousands of your products to see what's working and what isn't would be impossible. For this reason, we always say, 'Manage by exception.' By using the correct tags, you can receive a Google Analytics alert that tells you what your worst performing product and category pages are on your website for any given time period.

We don't like to do this alone however. We encourage each of our clients to take ownership of their merchandise and take a look at these statistics each week.

TAKING OWNERSHIP

This is your website, after all, and if these products are meaningful to you and you're passionate about your business, sometimes you might be the only one who knows exactly why certain products or pages are failing so badly. Maybe the images don't bring the item to life or the price point may be too high or the most important feature isn't mentioned. Focus on the top ten worst pages, because that's where you're losing the most potential sales.

We like to pretend my worst performing page is the only impression a potential customer has of my website. What would they think of my business and my product if they only landed on this one page? By asking yourself this question and treating each page like a 'first impression' opportunity, you'll be able to take your website to a new level.

By working on the poor performing pages, you'll invest your time and money in the right area and make a difference in your add-to-basket KPI. And, worst-case scenario, you'll be able to decide whether a product doesn't really fit with your website and if you should pull it for good.

Remember the bricks and mortar analogy we talked about earlier? How would you feel if someone walked into your High Street shop, saw your products on the shelves and immediately walked out? You'd want to know why!

CHECKING MIDDLE REVIEWS AND RATINGS

What if you cannot figure out how to improve your value proposition?

Another hidden gem that we track are middle-user reviews. Each Monday, we ask our clients to look at all the reviews they are getting and categorise them into different sections based on what they are about, like:

- Pricing.
- Packaging.
- Delivery.
- Website ease of use.
- Customer service.

Depending on the week and the client, there may be ten or more categories being addressed. Once this is done, we tell our clients to look for the middle reviews, or the ones that have a two or three out of five rating.

These middle-of-the-road reviews offer the most constructive and useful feedback, in our experience. Four- and five-star reviews often say everything is brilliant, which can be good for the ego but not so good when it comes to figuring out what changes you can make to improve your website, products or user experience. Extremely low ratings (one star) are often derogatory comments towards your website or staff. The middle reviews are what you want to look at. These offer the most useful information, both the good and the bad.

Look at 'middle review ratings' as a hidden source of improvements

WHERE TO INVEST
A CASE STUDY

Once you have the knowledge of your top worst performers, now it's important to decide where exactly to invest your money to make the biggest impact.

Here's a quick example that perfectly illustrates how this all works together and why KPIs are so critical:

Example story – invest in add to basket

- Online Health Sports supplement company - worried about their checkout. – it actually had a very healthy checkout to order stat of 85%. Pretty Good! Invest here and make £10,000 a year…. But looking at the add to basket stat of less than 6%..not good and very below average – invest here and make £500,000 a year…

- Normally this is the case for the 1st year a client comes to us

Here we have an online health supplement company that came to us and said, 'Hey, we're really worried about our checkout. We heard the checkout is the easiest way to improve revenue.'

When we had a look at their stats, we were able to easily discover what part of the sales process would be the most beneficial.

LET'S REVIEW

Remember, we are checking all stats against the following facts that we covered earlier.

On average:

✓ 11% of visitors will add a product to their basket.

✓ Of that 11%, 55% will proceed to checkout.

✓ Of that 55%, 84% will place an order.

They actually weren't lagging in the checkout-to-order rate because they were at a healthy 85% checkout-to-order ratio.

On the other hand, their add-to-basket rate was 6%, which was less than half of what it should be. This is where to invest. If they would have tried to improve their checkout to order, they may have made an extra 10 grand a year. But by investing the same amount of money in the area where they were lagging so far behind average stats, which was their add-to-basket ratio, they could end up gaining half a million in revenue annually.

Now, this is just one example and every client is different. Maybe you do need to invest in your checkout to order. That's why using all the KPIs is so critical.

FIND THE WORST-PERFORMING SEARCHES

Another thing to think about when investing in add-to-basket KPI is your website search. Using Google Analytics, you can actually track what visitors are looking for. It works well for B2C (business to consumer) and B2B (business to business) websites as well.

Search

- We've found that an average :
  - B2C site the search is used 6% by all traffic
  - B2B site, the search is used 16% by all traffic
  - Search should convert x4 your normal conversion rate

6% Of traffic should use search

x4 Is the conversion rate multiple (from no search) you should achieve

Add to Basket % KPI 1 of 3

smart**ebusiness**™ *The Magento Growth Specialists* 'Best Web and Digital Agency 2012' - *Direct Commerce Magazine* Magento

Most e-commerce platforms onsite search is rather poor out-of-the-box, but there are many ways in which it can be improved. When tracking this information, you can easily see things like your search exits, which is essentially your bounce rate. You'll also be able to look at the search refinement or people who are looking for a product and immediately changing their original search, refining it so it is more specific to what they want. For instance, your potential customer may search for a blue jumper at first but then refine their search quickly to a navy-blue jumper.

Just as you'll be doing with the product and category pages, you want to look at the top ten worst-performing searches. Let's say you had a unique search of over 100 in a week. Look for the lowest conversion rate, and you'll easily be able to see where your weakest searches are.

Seeing this should prompt you to action. It would be the equivalent of a customer walking into a shop on High Street and asking, 'Do you have this product?' Even though you say, 'Yes, we do!' the customer immediately turns around and walks out of the store without buying the product. This would scare most shop owners. They would wonder what was wrong:

✓ Is the product in the wrong colour?
✓ Is it the wrong size?
✓ Is it the wrong price?
✓ Was it too hard to locate?

By looking at the conversion rate, you'll know what products to look at so you can make the right changes to increase your add-to-basket KPI.

To improve you website's search, use some third-party improvements. Many can really dive into your customers' searches and better track your business. Options are available for creating your own search system within your site, tagging popular searches and linking Google Analytics to your store. Tagging popular searches can help you provide customers with trending search options, which many emotional-purchase buyers are looking for. The Google Analytics APWE linked to your site can help you construct category pages that work based on each page's value.

BROWSER ABANDONMENT— AN EASY/QUICK WIN

Browser abandonment. Behavioural and abandonment messaging is a quick and easy way to increase revenue by up to 10% on average, just by nudging them along in their journey through your website.

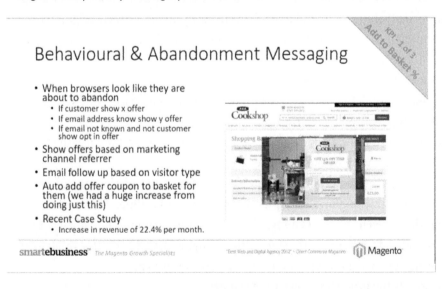

Browser abandonment tools help encourage visitors to take the next step and the next, until the sale is complete. Essentially, a pop-up comes on the screen when the mouse moves to exit the browser page. This is especially helpful with new customers, who are much less likely to add something to their basket than a returning customer. They don't know you and don't know if they can trust you or your products yet, so you have to work a little bit harder to motivate them to complete the checkout. Behavioural and abandonment messaging determines automatically when a new customer enters the site and can provide them with a new customer discount, such as 20% or 30% off their purchase, especially if they are moving their mouse towards abandonment. At the same time, it can tell if a customer is a returning one and offer a completely different promotion or none at all. Through our experience with browser abandonment, a simple yet precisely placed pop-up can result in higher revenues.

By using a tool like ScentTrail, you can target different segments with different offers. For instance, new customers get 10% off with free delivery but existing customers might only get free delivery.

A PRODUCT PAGE DESIGN CHECKLIST

So you can get quickly started optimising the raising of your add-to-basket KPI, here's the checklist we use to quickly find any friction points on the product page. Go through this list with your product page in front of you and see how many items you need to fix. This checklist came together as the result of many split tests we have run when optimising the add-to-basket KPI.

1. A common mistake is not putting the Add to Basket button above the fold, i.e. making a user scroll to see the Add to Basket button on some of the most used screen dimensions. Make sure the product options and Add to Basket button is shown first then the description.

2. Delivery information should be clearly displayed near the Add to Basket button. It's no good having it in the header or footer. It needs to be where the person is looking. Delivery should mention that it's free (if it is) and how fast it is.

3. Reviews should be prominently displayed underneath the product title or near the title. Again, where people are looking. Reviews should be done via a reputable third-party review system, e.g. Feefo, Trustpilot, etc. Show the number of reviews and invite people to read them.

4. Images should be large and be done well.

5. If the item is jewellery or something that is hard to work out the scale

of, have one photo that has the item next to a hand or something people know the size of. This way people can understand how big it is.

6. Make sure there is more than one image—a lifestyle shot, close-up shots, etc.

7. In stock declaration. This should be bold and noticeable in the key eye focus area. If stock is particularly important to a person, i.e. when they 'need it now,' make the stock icon dynamic so it looks like it's looking up the item in the warehouse and then showing it in stock.

8. On the product page underneath the buying information or description, we tend to lose people who the product is not quite right for. So show 'see other products in this category.' For example, if you are selling Gore-Tex hiking boots and the person is on an Adidas Gore-Tex Hiking Boot product page, then show links for 'see other Gore-Tex Boots' and 'see other Adidas Boots,' etc. This will keep them on the site rather than hitting the Back button back to Google.

9. The description should not include any words that people might not have in their vocabulary. Anything hard will shift their thinking to system 2 thinking and we don't want people to think yet.

10. Make the Add to Basket button clickable even if people have not selected the quantity yet. Don't grey it out until they have selected quantity. If they click it too early, then show them a message telling them they must add quantity. If you grey it out people won't see it and they might think it's out of stock.

HOW TO RAISE THIS KPI—ADD TO BASKET RATE

But how can you add to your basket rate?

BOUNCE RATE AND ADD TO BASKET

The add-to-basket stat is absolutely linked to the bounce rate. If they don't add anything to the basket, eventually they will leave the site and disappear (and the page they leave on is called the bounce page). The add-to-basket and bounce rates go very much hand in hand. A bounce rate is simply an exit: a hard, cold exit from the site without doing anything else (e.g. clicking back on the browser button and going back to Google Shopping). As ever (and with all these KPIs), if you compare what's happening online to a physical bricks-and-mortar store, it's easy to see why they are important. In this case, consider the following. A customer walks into a retail shop and starts browsing; they would start to browse the general sections of the shop (these we can call the categories). It's only after this they would start looking at individual products; they might then pick a product up and look at it more closely (or in a fashion store, they might try it on). If they decide they don't like the product and walk out of the shop, the equivalent of this behaviour online would be a bounce. So the first thing to consider is, did they bounce off the category or the product page?

We have four major places visitors can bounce: the home page, the category page, the product page and your search results pages. We're always going to get some of this behaviour; for example, just like a physical store, lots of people leave the store without buying. So it's useful to know how many should be leaving, i.e. what's normal. So let's define this:

Overall (across the entire site) the bounce rate on desktop devices should be less than 30% and for tablet/mobile less than 50%. So, let's call that 40% on average. If the bounce rate is higher, then reducing this and getting more engagement on the site is the first priority. Next, the category pages. They should not be bouncing more than 50%, followed by the product pages, which shouldn't bounce more than 60%. These are the critical stats to consider. All e-commerce sites are slightly different (and bounce stats vary, mostly according to the buying window, i.e. the average amount of time to buy), but in general, these suggested stats are very useful. To confirm, they are:

- Home page—less than 25% bounce.
- Category page—less than 50% bounce.
- Product page—less than 60% bounce.
- Overall—less than 40% bounce.
- Search exits—less than 20% bounce.

BOUNCE ON HOME PAGE

Home pages should be bouncing less than 25%. If you're losing more than this, then something is seriously wrong with your value proposition, or your traffic sources are completely irrelevant.

Home pages are not what they once were. Because of the growth of paid search channels driving visitors to product and category pages, the home page can often be seen quite far down the funnel. There is no one-page-fits-all method here, and the elements mainly depend on whether you are selling rational, problem-solving products (e.g. car battery) or emotional, spontaneous ones (e.g. a summer dress). In each case, the home page should focus on squashing the main anxieties of the shopper; for example, for the rational, problem-solving purchases, it should show massive reassurance promises and focus very much on the methodical buyers—all their problems will be solved by buying from here, all anxiety will evaporate. Whereas with the emotional, spontaneous shoppers it should inspire and make the shopper feel they are going to be transformed into a wonderful lifestyle by buying from this website. In fact, this is true throughout the entire website, and these two different buying characteristics will feature in a large part of the remainder of this book.

BOUNCE ON CATEGORY

Check bounce rate on the category pages as a whole—on average, this should be less than 50%; if overall average is higher than 55%, then look at each category individually (good idea to do this even if bounce is lower than 55%).

You will find that certain categories affect the overall bounce rate much more than others. Focus on the top categories by exits from the site; split test to increase engagement of these pages, especially if they are large SEO landing pages.

A high overall bounce on the category indicates bad merchandising, so implement the visual merchandising tool with simple rules to start (out of stock to the bottom, bestsellers to the top).

Individual bounces for categories which are high indicate a generally poor category. Common reasons include:
- The images are poor.
- The selection is poor.
- Not enough products.
- The prices are too high.

- Order of products is wrong, i.e. poor selling products at the top (top two rows are crucial).
- Poor filtering.
- Pagination (page numbers) too restrictive, so visitors can only see a small number: they like to view all, so consider lazy loading; consider split testing removing the sub categories from the navigation and letting visitors easily view all.
- Poor header image that doesn't frame the collection.

BOUNCE ON PRODUCT PAGE

This metric has become much more important with Google Shopping driving a lot more traffic to individual product pages. The visitors no longer go from the home to category to product page; they come directly from Google Shopping and land straight on this page, so it's a critical page to get right. The product pages are the new landing pages. This has made it slightly easier in some respects because it means we can tailor messages more specifically on the product pages, rather than the home page trying to do everything.

Objective of the product page is to get them to either . . .
- Add to basket.
- Continue on their selection process journey (it's highly likely that this is not quite the right product for them, and they want to see more products; if you don't help them do this, they will bounce off, back to Google).

Check bounce on product page—should be less than 60% on average.

Likely that product page bounces fluctuate widely between products; this is normal.

To reduce overall bounce on product page . . .
- Spontaneous buyers stay at the top, so make critical buying actions at the top:
    » Price should be at the top and visible.

> » Delivery reassurances should be at the top; for example, order now and receive tomorrow, September 3.
> » Add to Basket buttons big and high above the fold.
> » Availability of product should be clear.
> » Critical reassurances (if not too cluttered, e.g. free returns should be above the fold).

- Bigger and better images always help.
- Open out all the tabs so people can scroll easily.
- Include related categories and attributes that this product is in.
- Include related searches this product is in.
- Consider adding scarcity to stock, for example, 'only a few left.'
- Implement improved reviews system.
- Implement Q&A system.
- Customers trust the reviews and the Q&A more than the actual description, so make them visible and open as default.
- Decrease page load time of landing page—if you segment your bounce traffic in Google Analytics and look at the page load time it's often higher than the average. This can indicate that page load is an issue.

A high individual product page bounce can commonly be caused by:
- Poor image.
- Out of stock.
- Price too high.
- Delivery time not clear or too slow.
- Poor product name.

BOUNCE AND SEARCH (INTERNAL)

- Internal searches for B2C should be 8% of overall traffic; B2B should be 15%+ of internal traffic. If use of internal search is less than these % then this is often due to bad positioning of the search box on the site. Onsite search is a great engagement device and leads to big conversion rate increases.
- Search conversion should have a 4× increase over normal conversion. If the conversion rate of those using internal search is not 4×, then invest

in your search tool and manually look at the results pages of your top search terms—redirect these to the best page on the site. If people are searching for products that are out of stock or not sold, take them to an information page explaining what has happened and the replacement products.

- Search exits should be less than 20%—if more than 20% of internal searchers are leaving then you need to review site search using a tool like Mouseflow. What are people searching for, what are they seeing, why are they leaving? What experience would be better for them?

- Add popular searches above the search box—many of the spontaneous buyers need help knowing what to search for, so showing popular search terms on pages can trigger an engagement and the start of a sale.

- Add related searches in the search results dropdown—as people type a search show them what others searched for.

- Add 'other people searched for' on the search results page—when the search page loads, to reduce exits show what others searched for, hence making it easier for them to continue rather than leaving.

- KPI create a custom Google Analytics report that sends every Monday to show the highest search terms by exits, then you can set up a system to check these search terms each week and tweak the search results pages.

The add-to-basket rate is all about convincing someone that they want to buy the item. Increasing the desirability and the sellability of the item is going to put many more people into your e-commerce sales funnel.

The add-to-basket rate is not just about the numbers, you have to add a little sales magic to the process. You need to hone your inner magician.

When we see Derren Brown on TV, he seems like a crazy demigod, bending people's minds to his will.

Of course, behind the scenes, there must be many failures where Derren says, 'Do this,' and the subject says, 'No way, Mr Brown, you're a weirdo.'

But do you think Derren could become a good conversion rate optimiser? Yes, of course!

Here are some of the techniques that he uses in his performances that we can swipe and deploy on our e-commerce sites.

1. **Focus on those likely to buy.** Like any good hypnotist, he starts with a large group of people and then whittles down to the most suggestive of participants, i.e. he gets rid of the tyre kickers. On our website when analysing

data, we first need to remove from our analysis those that will never buy. There's no point watching hundreds of session recordings of people who bounced on the site in under 30 seconds.

Instead, we need to focus on the highest potential and the first segment I look at is the 'almost buyers'—people that spend a long time on the website but don't buy. These are the most suggestible group who have the capacity to double your conversion rate.

2.   Gain rapport with the subject. Derren uses techniques to gain instant trust because he wants the subject to relax and let their guard down. Techniques like:

- Find out where the person is from and say their grandparent is from that town.
- That they went to the same college.
- Say their mother or father shares the same name as them.

On an online store, we can do this with personalisation, by tailoring the home page based on their recent purchases. Shopify and Amazon do this well with 'because you listened to Jimi Hendrix Blues you might like' . . . you feel they care more about you than you'd feel from a generic bestseller page.

Also, if you have the data you can tailor the 'Mark in Oxford just bought this' type notifications to only show people who have similar names and similar locations to their IP address, i.e. if we can show people they relate to more who have bought, then we will have much more success than just showing random people are buying.

3.   Act for a small commitment. Like Cialdini, Derren knows that asking a person to make a big commitment from a cold start is too much of a big step. So he uses small actions in the direction of the behaviour he ultimately wants the person to take. He does not ask them to push a person off a roof immediately; instead, he asks them to commit small misdemeanours first.

On many stores we have split tested putting prices on the home page and not. Often no pricing information works better. This is because we are asking for a sale too early. We need a smaller step first. A great deal of sites make use of an engagement device in the form of a home page wizard or survey (see Naked Wines for a good example www.nakedwines.com). We know if we can get people interacting with a survey, using site search or just starting moving forward towards the checkout, then we will increase conversion.

4.   Social proof. In the Derren Brown murder show, he gets his subjects to arrive at a black-tie event underdressed. They are NOT part of the crowd, and this is uncomfortable. Social exclusion is one of our biggest fears.

The flip side of this is social inclusion. On a website, we must show there is a buzz around the brand and website that people can gain access to by becoming a customer. This leads on to social media marketing and careful placement of social proof along their journey. Also remarketing should not be just 'you looked at this product, buy it'; instead, we should weave in social proof of a big group of like-minded buyers that they can and want to be part of.

5.   Time constraint. Again, in his recent murder show on Netflix, where people are brought to the point where some of them commit murder, he introduces a time constraint to induce action. Adding a time constraint forces the brain to reduce its focus to the immediate situation and thus find a solution to that problem.

Luckily, we are not trying to get people to do something horrific. However, we can use time constraints to illicit action. Countdown timers on delivery or offers do work as do loyalty programs with points that are 'about to run out.' Many of our retailers have had great success with Amazon Prime-type services where people pay to get free delivery for a period. As the time starts running out, the conversion rate increases.

HOW A PRISONER INCREASED MY E-COMMERCE SALES

To increase the desire to add the products to the basket, we can learn a lot from great advertising copywriters. One of our favourites is the late Gary Halbert.

Gary Halbert was one of those rogue copywriters who could print money just using words.

But his life was constantly up and down, millionaire one minute and destitute the next.

One down period landed him in white-collar jail.

It was during this time that he wrote to his son Boron each week and taught him marketing via a series of letters.

It's our good fortune that these letters are now published online as *The Boron Letters*, and anyone can read them for free.

They are a little dated in terms of media, mostly focusing on direct mail advertising, but marketing messaging never changes.

We are still trying to sell to the same human brain which has not altered its fundamental needs and desires for millions of years.

Personally, we learnt a lot from reading the letters and started using this on the e-commerce sites we manage.

Here are some key insights we took from the letters to apply to e-commerce.

- People are nervous of being sold to, and Gary used handwritten envelopes to get past the rubbish bin. In e-commerce on the home page we need to sell less and attract engagement more. People are not ready to buy on the home page; instead, we must invite people on a journey.

- Personalisation is key. Gary made a lot of money sending out the famous 'coat of arms' letter. This letter was personalised to the person's surname. On an e-commerce store people want to have the site and home page personalised to them so that it becomes a lot more useful. A personal shopping approach really helps them decide on what to buy.

- Gary recommended writing out the most successful adverts of all time. I wrote out and copied famous adverts selling Mercedes, perfume, books, etc. Doing this, I started to see things I couldn't see when reading the adverts; writing them out really focused my attention. I noticed the flow, the repetition of key points and the overall voice. Applying this to e-commerce means I study the successful competitors of my clients; I buy from them, pay for user testing on competitors' sites and scan them for structure. I basically slow myself down, so I start noticing exactly what is going on.

- The author and voice/tone of the writer is important. Gary taught me that the person telling the story and writing the copy has a large impact on the subsequent sale. People buy from people they trust, admire, are like them or want to be. With e-commerce adding a personal voice to the website, such as personal guarantees and expert tips and named customer managers, it adds another layer which increases the conversion rate.

- Testimonials are important. Customers' stories are key to selling, and they are much more powerful if they come from people like the buyer. With e-commerce, we can start personalising the reviews that people see to be from similar locations to the buyer.

One of Gary's students was John Carlton, and he introduced us to 'customer detective work.'

Many e-commerce sites totally murder their conversion rates by writing poor copy and not fitting offers to customer desires.

John Carlton, the legendary copywriter, does something called undercover detective work when putting together a new sales letter.

John knows that talking to the director of a company and asking them how to sell the product is pretty much useless. Of course, he does talk to the director as he's the one paying the bills, but it's very rare that something great comes from this conversation.

So what is this undercover work?

It's about talking to customers, talking to frontline sales staff, and looking at reviews and really getting into the shoes of the customers. The trouble is, as soon as you talk to them they start freezing up.

A good example is when a recent new client invited us to lunch to talk about their site. We sat down, all relaxed, and he was talking about his company and his passion; it was great stuff. But as soon as we got back to the office and started trying to increase his conversion rate, he clammed up and started speaking like a textbook. He didn't realise that when he relaxed his natural automatic sales pitch came out, but when he tried to do it consciously it was constrained and false.

So when writing sales copy for products or emails, we need to make sure that we are talking to the right people and secondly that they are relaxed and not aware that we are making notes.

We need to get access to the subconscious, intuitive flow that the top sales people have.

Look at your own phone sales team; there is always one person who can outsell everyone else. But asking them how they sell is like asking them what the back of their head looks like. They cannot see it. To get the gems out of the sales star and to translate that into a sales script and product copy, you need to record them. Record them until they forget they are being recorded.

Also, when talking to customers, get them relaxed. Don't ask them why they bought; instead, talk to them about something else, perhaps what they thought of a recent email. Get them relaxed and then subtly get them talking about their recent purchase. We must get at the unconscious decision maker inside every customer if we want to be able to craft incredible copy and powerful offers.

BECOME A SPY

Going further with the undercover metaphor and widening it to the whole website experience is important because you really need to get a handle on how a customer views your e-commerce offering.

Everyone wants to understand other people and that's why people seem to like body swap movies. You know those movies like Tom Hanks's *Big*, *Vice Versa*, or more recently *The Change-Up*, *Jumanji*, etc., where they use a genie or magic to accidentally swap bodies.

Comedy ensues—perhaps we all hanker to try out someone else's life, if only just briefly. If you Google 'Body Swap Movies,' there have been hundreds of movies like this.

Hollywood knows that we like to see different people experience other people's lives.

Of course, these movies always end with a cheesy part where people agree to understand each other more and have a better relationship. But that's just the narrative. What interests us is the experience of jumping into someone else's shoes.

Marketers like us always say things like 'jump into the customer's shoes.'

Or . . .

'think like the customer.'

And whilst this is true, it's very hard to get out of our own head and truly see what a prospect sees. Quite often we are in a completely different physical and environmental place.

There was a program running recently called *Undercover Boss* where the boss put on a disguise and went into the workplace. No matter which company did this, there were always fundamental problems raised at each location, stuff that you would have thought would have been obvious—but it took a silly wig and some false teeth to *see* the real picture.

With e-commerce, we can't go and work on the cash register and pretend to be a shop assistant.

So what do we do to get into the customer's mindset?

Here are some suggestions:

- Use a service like 'whatusersdo' and pick typical customer demographics and ask them to make a purchase on your store. Listen to what they struggle with.

- Listen to customer service calls or sales calls. Start your day listening to two or three of these, and you will pick up at least one or two gems a week.
- Read your reviews, especially your middle reviews.

Pay attention to when you feel emotion about what customers are saying or writing. Often the places where we have the most self-deception are the areas where we feel emotion.

You can also pay for 'whatusersdo' to visit your competitors' sites to see how their experience is on those sites. This is especially good to do if you know the competitor is crushing it on AdWords.

WHY THE BOUNCE RATE DOESN'T BOUNCE

Reducing the bounce rate is all about keeping the visitors on your site.

The bounce rate is quite a confusing metric because it should be called the non-engagement rate.

When we think of a bounce, we picture a ball hitting the floor and immediately bouncing back. But with a visitor, they can remain on the page for an indefinite time and still be classed as a bounce.

Why is this?

A bounce on a website is classified as a user that visited your website and took no further action, i.e. didn't click on anything.

If you ran a blog, a high bounce rate might be okay, i.e. people come and read an article and then leave. This would be classed as a bounce, but it could be fine.

This is not the case with an e-commerce site as a visitor that makes no further clicks is a visitor who has no chance of buying.

So how do we improve the e-commerce bounce rate?

The first thing to do is to look at your site page load speed in Google Analytics. Next use a segment to show bounced traffic and note the page load speed for these visitors. If the average page load speed is significantly higher for bounced traffic, this means that a slow site has a large factor in the bounce rate.

Basically, some of your visitors are encountering a slow loading page, and these people can't be bothered to wait. They know that it takes at least six minutes to find and buy something and on a slow site this could be tripled, and they would rather be doing something else.

So check site speed first.

Secondly, bounce rate is going to affect both SEO and paid traffic. When someone bounces, they invariably hit the Back button, and this takes them back to Google. Google makes a note of searches who return from clicking on a search ranking and gives it a little minus point. Get enough minus points, and you will see less SEO and paid traffic. Instead, Google will push websites that tend to get clicked on and don't bounce back.

For key SEO landing pages, you want to be split testing for engagement. Find your top five SEO landing pages and split test the images on the page or the first words seen on the page. The SEO landing page could be a blog page or category, and both have images and titles to experiment with. Increase the engagement of these pages and you will see more traffic.

For product pages, a common bounce is due to a user searching for one thing, e.g. Gore-Tex Walking Shoes, and then landing on a Gore-Tex Shoe but not exactly the shoe they want to buy. They want to see other models. With no choice they click back to Google and another product. But if we give them the option to see 'related categories,' that is 'see other Gore-Tex Shoes' then they click on this rather than the Back button.

We have split tested related category links with good success and tend to position the link under the product image.

Another way to reduce product bounce rates is to take people to a category-style landing page where the product they are interested in is made large at the top. They see the product they are interested in but can see other products underneath.

This style of product landing page works well on sites where the initial product landing page is different from the final product bought. If the product bought is different from the landing page 20% of the time, then this technique can work well. You can work this out easily in Google Analytics.

RECAP: ADD-TO-BASKET RATE

Your product pages are just as, if not more, important than your category pages, especially when using Google Shopping. Make sure all essential details and the

Add to Basket button is above the fold, provide info about other similar items and make sure customers can easily return to previous products they were looking at.

KPI: ADD-TO-BASKET RATE

Put it to use:
- 11% of visitors should be adding to their baskets. If your percentage is less than 11%, this KPI needs attention.
- Determine your type of buyer: spontaneous, methodical, humanistic or competitive.
- Adjust your product pages so that all pertinent information occurs above the fold. This makes it easier for customers to see everything and make quick decisions.
- Look at the middle reviews to determine what your site is doing wrong.
- Improve your worst-performing searches to increase add-to-basket rate.

Answer the following questions:
- What type of buyer does your website appeal to? Why?
- Take a look at your product pages and category pages. What areas can you improve on?
- What is your worst-performing search? Why do you think it performs so poorly?
- Take a look at your middle reviews. What areas do these reviews indicate need work? Write out your plan for improvement here.

*See back of book for all of our recaps and step-by-step instructions for KPIs all in one handy workbook.

WEBSITE SPEED
AND CAPACITY

The website speed and capacity KPI looks at the current speed of your website. As you are aware, page speed is vital for a couple of reasons. First is user experience. Each quarter of a second it takes for your page to load begins to paint a negative picture in the mind of your site visitor. Slow page load can mark your business as unreliable or behind the times in the mind of your potential customer. Each small negative thought can add up to your visitor looking elsewhere to fill their order.

The second reason, of course, is page ranking. Google and other search engines use page load speed as a determining factor and will penalise sites that don't make speed a priority, especially for mobile.

There are a couple of ways you can benchmark your site's current performance. A handy website, www.webpagetest.org, is an excellent online tool to measure website speed.

You can also use Google Analytics:
✓ Sign in to Google Analytics.
✓ Navigate to your view.
✓ Open reports.
✓ Select behaviour and then site speed.

Here, you want your site to register under four seconds. Between four and five is okay, but any higher and your website is getting slow. You especially want your landing pages to load quickly as this is a tangible factor in the first impression that is registered unconsciously by the visitor.

One of the most important considerations with this KPI is how fast your website is when under peak loads. It may be blazing fast on a normal day, but on holidays where it sees more traffic, and more potential revenue, you don't want it to come to a screeching halt. This KPI helps protect all of the other work you're doing, such as marketing and AdWords, and to make sure the website works when you need it to.

SLOW WEBSITES AND MENTAL FRICTION

Like we said above, the speed of your website plays an important role in the add-to-basket, basket-to-order, and proceed-to-checkout process. In a customer's subconscious, they have a specific length of time they allow themselves to spend on a website. If you have a slow website, and the customer cannot check out within that specific length of time they have allotted in their mind, that is where you'll see a lot of unexplained abandonment. If the website is slow, it is more likely to be a frustrating experience for the user.

For example, when we worked on GSF car parts, customers were originally on the site for six minutes. After making the website twice as fast, customers still spent six minutes on the site, but they purchased much more during that time because they could get more done in that amount of time. The average order value and conversion both went up.

WHEN TO TEST WEBSITE SPEED AND CAPACITY

Some websites do 80% of their sales during two months of the year. If that describes your business, then testing your website speed in August will likely produce brilliant numbers, but if it's not a peak moment, this test won't tell you how your site will do in the run-up to Christmas or on Black Friday/Cyber Monday.

The secret is to measure the load from the previous year, if available, and estimate what you think you'll need this year. Then always have a margin of safety. If you think you're going to have X number of visitors per minute, then you want to have 50% or more capacity available for them. When calculating what you'll need, also consider your marketing campaigns. Maybe your email campaign is going out with on-sale items at an already peak time. This additional traffic could bring the site to a halt. You need to be sure you have ample resources so your users can get more done in the amount of time they allow themselves to spend on the site.

Website speed and capacity is one of the most important KPIs. It affects every other part of your website, as well as the conversion rate. At smartebusiness, we've found many ways to increase the speed and capacity of a site, from varnish caching, optimising the server and using clean code.

RECAP: WEBSITE SPEED AND CAPACITY

Customers spend an average of six minutes on your website. If your site is running slow, they'll achieve a lot less in that amount of time than if it is running at a high speed. The faster your website speed, the higher your average order value and conversion rate will be.

KPI: WEBSITE SPEED AND CAPACITY

Put it to use:
- Slow page load can cause Google penalties that affect your page ranking.
- Measure your web speed often. This will help increase conversion rates.
- Google Analytics can help you measure your website speed, as well as other sites like www.webpagetest.org.
- Your site should measure under four seconds.
- Increasing speed and capacity involves using clean code, varnish caching and optimising the server.

Answer the following questions:
- Have you experienced slow page load recently or seen a lot of browser abandonment from visitors?
- What is your current website speed? Use the information in this chapter to check the speed via webpagetest.org and Google Analytics.
- What are three things that could be causing the reduction in website speed? How can you fix them?
- Are there certain times of the year when you need more website capacity (e.g. Black Friday, Christmas)?
- How do you plan on making sure your website is ready for visitors during this peak time?

*See back of book for all of our recaps and step-by-step instructions for KPIs all in one handy workbook.

HOW TO RAISE THIS KPI— WEBSITE SPEED AND CAPACITY

But what can you do about your site's capabilities?

MOBILE SPEED

- Do the mobile speed test here https://search.google.com/test/mobile-friendly Check for images that don't load quickly; how does Google rate you?
- Loading testing—ask your host to do some load testing on mobile above what you think you will need for your busiest period. When does the site load go below five seconds? This will be the point where conversion rate will start to be negatively affected.
- Implement a AMP mobile site: https://www.ampproject.org.

DESKTOP SPEED

- Load test the desktop site. When does the page load reduce below five seconds?
- Reduce image size and make sure that the admin team understand how to optimise images. Often we optimise a site and then two weeks later the client's team have unknowingly replaced home page images that slow the whole site down.
- Create page load speed alerts in Google Analytics, so that if page load increases over a certain threshold you get sent an email.
- Do page load speed tests on the top four websites listed on Google's natural search results for your biggest search keyword. Find out how quick they are and make sure you site is faster and as fast under load. Google will not send you more traffic if it knows your site is slow.

TABLET SPEED

- Look at the main tablets being used and their screen resolutions. Check the responsive site 'break points' to make sure each size is optimised for page load.

- Load test on tablets to highlight issues.

SPEED IN GENERAL

It's all about speed. Don't just think about speed in terms of page load, but think about how quickly your business reacts to a customer as it has a key impact on the conversion rate.

We humans think we are level-headed, consistent beings that don't change our minds from one minute to the next.

It's an illusion.

We are all over the place.

We think that we are rational, that our decisions make sense.

Alas, experiments have shown that we make some decisions subconsciously and then come up with a conscious reason for that choice afterwards.

Crazy! Our subconscious decides and then we pretend it was our idea.

So, when you have an interested prospect on your store you need to act with speed before the 'monkey mind' gets fixated on the next thing.

We have done a lot of AdWords for promotional product stores and they tend to do lead generation on product pages. It turns out that unless you respond within 10 minutes of that lead then the chances of closing that business reduce by 90%.

This is because people are only in the receptive zone for buying in that instant.

In that instant they are convinced they cannot live without the product or service you sell. Ten minutes later and they don't even remember visiting your site.

So how does this help us with e-commerce and selling physical products online?

Well, response rate to live chat, support emails and every interaction must be swift.

We need instant gratification. We need to:

- Help people on the checkout page within five seconds otherwise they will walk.

- Respond to contact enquiries within 10 minutes, otherwise doubts creep in.
- Have a fast website (under four seconds load time in Google Analytics).
- Deliver products faster than we promise.
- Upsell quickly whilst they are still in the 'buying zone.'
- Do not make people wait on phone lines.

Every interaction you have with the customer, whether it's digital or personal, needs to be fast and super attentive.

Time is king—we are all only in the buying zone for a small window.

LIFETIME CUSTOMER VALUE

LET'S LOOK AT
LIFETIME CUSTOMER VALUE

Lifetime customer value (LTCV) is the total revenue divided by the total number of customers. This will give you the average spend per customer. Many e-commerce businesses don't track this because it's not a metric you can pull from Google Analytics. However, focusing on this number is important.

LTCV allows you to track things like:

- Which products purchased by first-time customers lead to the highest lifetime value?
- How do discount coupons affect lifetime value?
- Which marketing channels generate the highest lifetime value?

We want to be recruiting customers that make growth downstream easier. Too many businesses focus on getting the first sale, totally ignoring the potential future sales that a customer can generate. If you sell furniture, for example, a good salesman knows that selling a customer a chair that is part of a set almost always guarantees the customer will come back and purchase the rest of the set. If you sell a chair by itself, however, you'll only get that one sale.

A big part of the LTCV KPI is the repeat customer rate. This is the average number of times a customer buys from your store. Some stores differ largely on this metric. A clothing website will see higher numbers here, but a lawnmower dealer would traditionally see a much lower number. It doesn't matter what this metric is when you start. What matters is seeing this KPI move up. If it moves down while all other metrics rise, the long-term growth of your business will eventually derail. In fact, all these seven KPIs work like this. For true business growth, you must see all rise together, or at least remain the same while the others rise. Raising one KPI at the expense of another might lead to a great month but build an unhealthy future. Consider Black Friday, for example. If it isn't approached the right way, it can kill your Christmas sales. These KPIs will show you why.

Some of the best ways to increase lifetime customer value are:

LOOK AT THE TYPE OF CUSTOMERS YOU'RE RECRUITING

Many businesses have products that naturally lead to a repeat purchase rate, and some customers are drawn to these items. For example, if you're selling supplements or contact lenses, these products lend themselves to repeat purchases. If you begin looking at the products you're selling, you'll begin to see which of your products have higher lifetime customer value. Armed with this information, you can feed it back into your recruitment activity, such as Google AdWords and Google Shopping. You might then start bidding slightly higher on the products that provide a higher LTCV.

Our product, ScentTrail, helps you obtain and track this information, getting it out of your e-commerce backend and into AdWords. As a result, you are able to recruit customers who are most likely to become repeat customers.

START LOOKING AT DELIVERY CHOICES

When your customers are ordering, what shipping rates are they choosing? Do most want their product immediately? Or do they choose to wait three to four days? Measure this against your LTCV. Are people who ship your products to their home quickly much more likely to come back and purchase again? If this is the case, you can take steps towards getting the products to them even sooner and increasing your lifetime customer value even more.

At smartebusiness, we tend to find that the 30 days directly following a purchase is a critical window to develop repeat customers. This, of course, doesn't apply to every website. Those that sell clothes, for instance, will cater to a certain percentage of impulse buyers and as-needed shoppers. LTCV can increase with these sites as well. You just have to create a positive experience that leaves the customer feeling satisfied. Remember, the purchase has a large emotional component.

CONSIDER THE COUPONS THEY USE

For this comparison, consider customers who make a purchase with a coupon and those who make a purchase without one. How does that affect how quickly they come back to make another purchase? This information can be a gold mine, helping you understand which factors actually increase the lifetime customer value. Once you know, you can use those factors to recruit more customers who have a high potential for repeat purchases.

CUSTOMER SATISFACTION

One of the most obvious, but necessary, ways to increase your lifetime customer value is to make sure that every customer is happy with their purchase. Read your reviews, benchmark them against your past reviews and against competitors. As you grow, make sure you are still maintaining this level of happiness. If you have a 4-1/2 star average when you're selling 10 items a day, you should still have that average when you're selling 1,000 items a day. If your average star rating drops, this means customers are no longer happy, and your lifetime customer value will drop. If it does, you will have a much harder time growing your business and increasing revenue.

If you're not sure how to cultivate overall customer satisfaction, consider offering a free gift to first-time buyers. Give them something they didn't expect. If they're buying a jacket, for instance, give them a pair of sunglasses as well. It's something inexpensive that has perceived value. You can even split test this by giving 50% of customers the free gift and the other 50% nothing to determine how it affects your LTCV.

USE REMARKETING TO MAKE YOUR SHOP FAMOUS

Why do brands like Mars spend millions of dollars making sure that we see their products all over the place? Why does Coca Cola make sure that we see their brand at events where we feel good?

It's obvious.

What we are familiar with we trust.

But why is this?

When the brain was developing the environment was a lot more dangerous. There were a lot more predators and people died a lot more frequently from normal day-to-day activities.

We had to survive in this environment, hence everything that was new was categorised as 'bad until proven otherwise.'

Let's say we were walking to the watering hole in the morning and saw a new type of bird. It's a large bird and we are not sure whether it's safe, so we proceed with caution.

Nothing happens that day and the bird just watches us.

The next day the same thing happens.

After a week of seeing the bird every day, we relax and understand the bird means no harm.

This is how we are wired. We treat new items with caution and only relax once we have seen the item many times and nothing has happened.

Repetition plus nothing happening equals trust.

Thus, when presented with a buying opportunity, we tend to reach for the brand that we trust and are familiar with.

This is not rocket science.

However, how can we afford to become familiar to our customers before they buy? We cannot sponsor the super bowl (not yet!).

But what we can do now with Facebook, Google, Twitter, etc., is carefully target people and become the 'repeat, repeat, repeat = safe' famous in that small niche.

We don't have to be famous for everyone, only a very small, select group of people.

Google Analytics recently launched a native predictor of buying intent right inside everyone's account. With this information we can remarket to the very small subset of people that we want to be famous for.

For these people we can be everywhere.

Forget the people that found the store by accident, forget the people who were checking out the competition. Focus on the people that show buying intent and Kardashian the crap out of them.

It doesn't even cost that much.

Inside every rock is a sculpture and inside every account's traffic are the potential buyers.

You just need to chisel them out and get famous.

But how do you actually get remarketing to work, i.e. how do we make online visitors actually buy?

When we first started marketing we realised we needed to get in front of prospective customers. That's obvious.

Clearly you need to be selling something that people need or want.

The next step is realising that you need to be much more persistent with your marketing, i.e. resend emails that have not been opened. Follow up with people that visited that didn't buy. Remarket on Facebook and Google to people that abandoned the site.

Be like a terrier that won't let go.

But if we miss one element in the above sequence we lose.

Many of the websites we get asked to look at are stuck in the above loop. They find people that are likely to buy, then they remarket and follow up.

However, nothing really happens.

Remarketing does not work. Return on ad spend is low.

They can't scale because they are missing the secret sauce.

So, what is this secret ingredient?

'Believable Proof.'

You must be able to demonstrate believable proof that your product takes the purchaser to where the buyer wants to be.

This cannot be done in your own voice. You cannot say to the prospect 'we are amazing' unless you yourself are a trusted celebrity or an accredited authority.

But you can create believable proof in the following ways.

- If you sell beauty products, remarketing to prospects with a Facebook post that has a ton of shares, likes, comments, and social proof from women just like them. But good social proof like this works with a lot of products.
- If you sell a medical ebook getting an endorsement from a doctor from a well-known university.
- If you sell car parts getting an endorsement from a Formula One mechanic.
- If you sell blinds getting an endorsement from a TV DIY personality.

If you don't have the budget for celebrity endorsement, then you need to use social media 'social proof' to create believable proof.

To do this, create Facebook Posts that tell the story of your product or show recent customers using the product. Then make these posts evergreen and buy a ton of social proof on these posts.

This way when your prospects see them they will think 'wow this product is the real deal, look at all these people who love this product.'

Don't forget the secret ingredient; without it is like trying to play tennis with no strings in your racquet.

But before you can create proof, you need to make sure that you are creating proof about something your customers actually care about.

When you start out, you will have some idea of what you need to prove with your product. You could be thinking:

- Can you prove you can get this delivered on time and in one piece?

- Does this product work?
- I need to prove my product is better than the competition.

We must start with something; however, to really hit the jackpot we need to listen.

Who to?

You know those annoying loud, shouty people that comment on your Facebook ads that this product is a scam, or not as good as *x*, *y*, *z*. Or perhaps they buy your product and then moan about it on Feefo or Trustpilot.

These people are inconveniently essential to your marketing efforts.

Inconvenient because they are annoying.

However, for every loud person there will be 80 people who think something similar but are too British to say anything.

These loud people are telling you the main objections that people have to your product.

Every time someone complains or trolls you, make a note of it in a little spreadsheet, categorise them and put a count against each one.

When you have your main objections, you can get to work.

For example, perhaps you are selling baby sleeping bags and the main troll comment you get is about how these bags are not better than a cot duvet for helping a baby sleep. Next you would need to answer the following question:

How can I, without a shadow of a doubt in the prospect's mind, prove to them that our baby sleeping bags are the best sleeping solution and a clear choice over the competition?

Here's how you might answer that question:

- Ask recent customers for testimonials on how improved their child's sleep is with your product.
- Employ a doctor and scientist to take some measurements of a sleeping child in your sleeping bag compared to a normal duvet. Show the difference in restlessness over a night's sleep. Ask the scientist and doctor to endorse the study and the product.
- Ask recent customers to specifically talk about their worries about the objection before purchase and how they are now free of the objection.
- Use an evergreen Facebook post that you get a ton of social proof on and has a lot of people commenting that 'this is the most amazing sleep

product ever' and then use this as a remarketing post to traffic that comes to the site.
- Use video testimonials on the product page, with mums talking about before and after experiences.

Okay, so now we are starting to see what real marketing is. It's not some quick trick but a carefully planned out sequence of believable proof that overcomes the prospects' main objection in a predictable and automated way.

USE CUSTOMER LISTS IN GOOGLE ADWORDS

Uploading your customer email list to Google AdWords is an excellent way to increase LTCV. Once you upload the list, you can choose to have Google show your ad or website to anyone on your list who searches for a product related to your business. Uploading your list also lets you bid on much more generic terms that you wouldn't bid on for regular Google traffic. For instance, if you're selling casters for chairs, you wouldn't normally bid on casters. It's too broad. In this instance, however, if you have a past customer that purchased casters from you, you'd want to bid on that keyword.

Using RLSA (remarketing lists for search ads) helps cultivate repeat customers, reminding them of the good experience they had with you. Remarketing can be looked at as a type of marketing training for your clients. It's easy to forget about a place you've shopped at once, maybe on a whim or during a busy holiday season. When combined with promos or discount coupons, remarketing can expose those first-time buyers to the benefits of being brand loyal.

DIG INTO YOUR STATISTICS

While you might work hard to keep all of your customers on regular buying cycles, some will turn into lapsed customers. Digging into your statistics will help you understand which ones have become lapsed—which means they haven't purchased from you in 12–18 months and the probability of them buying from you in the future is low. With this information, you can create an offer that will help you increase the spend potential of this type of buyer. By giving these lapsed customers an offer you wouldn't give your current customers, or those who would readily purchase from you at a higher rate and with your current model, you can increase your revenue across the board. Information like this keeps you from having to make a trade-off, like offering a discount to everyone just to motivate a small section of your buying audience.

TRACK AGAINST MARKETING CHANNELS

Tracking each marketing channel helps you understand where your best customers are coming from and which channel is increasing your lifetime customer value. Are customers coming in from SEO or from AdWords? If they're coming in from AdWords, you can even dive in and find which campaign is having the most success. With this information, you can recruit more customers with high lifetime customer values. For instance, instead of your normal return on spend for each area, you might lower your return on spend for those channels that are increasing the LTCV so that you can recruit more customers that will come back throughout the year and buy more of your products.

ScentTrail allowed us to track LTCV via marketing channels. It also allows us to see what effect the initial marketing offer had on LTCV. For example, if we're looking at 10% OFF vs. 20% OFF, what would be the effect on the LTCV? We know as we've tested it across multiple clients. The answer is not nearly as much as you would expect.

It's important to note that many of our clients have a problem with discounting, simply because they don't want their website to be known as a discount store. To make sure this doesn't happen, we recommend making each discount look as if it's the only one being offered. This way, visitors believe they are getting the best price—and everyone else has to pay full price. Some websites also avoid discounting because they believe it will affect their LTCV negatively; many think that customers will only purchase products when they are discounted. This is not the case.

The trick is finding the middle ground which is being able to discount but doing it covertly and never looking like a discount site. For example, one website that sells contact lenses changes the pricing it offers in the Google Shopping channel to undercut competition and it does this dynamically. However, if you were to visit the contact lens store via the home page you would see a different price, i.e. this store is discounting where it needs to, in order to get the sale, but charging a higher price where there is less friction. We have also used similar strategies when a manufacturer has a large wholesale business and wants to start a direct channel. To get the direct model off the ground you need to have good offers to beat the wholesale market, but as soon as you do the wholesale channel freaks out. So you have to proceed with caution and only show the discounts to traffic that is most likely not your wholesalers coming to check on your pricing.

The critical thing here is to not look like a discounter, to make the visitor believe that most people are paying full price and that they are one of the few getting a deal. This middle ground is one of the most profitable strategies you can run in your e-commerce store.

Lifetime customer value is an excellent figure to watch year on year, and a KPI that will help you grow your business. Use these tips to track it and increase it.

GET FEEDBACK FROM YOUR CUSTOMERS

Ask Them When They Are High. It's frustrating to see thousands of people visit your site never to return.

It's even more annoying when you have paid for them to come and have a look.

We desperately need to know why they are not buying. What can I do differently?

But if you ask them, they won't tell you. Why should they? It's not their job to improve your website, and they are busy finding a product that fits their needs.

So how do we find out what to improve? We ask them when they are high.

Just after buying something, we get a 'buyers high,' a shot of dopamine that makes us feel good. This is when to ask customers how we can improve the site.

Not only do they feel good, but they have finished their main task and are okay answering questions. But surely the people who have just bought don't need anything fixed on the site? After all, they are the buyers.

Yes, but the lowest hanging fruit any e-commerce site has is the 'almost buyers,' the people that get most of the way to the checkout but then bail.

These almost buyers will be very similar in mindset to the actual buyers. Thus, what annoys the buyers will annoy the almost buyers.

We have a feedback question running now on one of our biggest sites and the information coming in is priceless.

USE A THANK-YOU CAMPAIGN

People like to feel appreciated, this is clear.

With e-commerce we tend to thank people after they buy on the order success page and in the order confirmation email.

However, given that everyone does this customers don't see it as they expect it.

To convey our gratitude for their order we must go one step further and set a remarketing thank-you campaign.

Why?

Two reasons.

One, we want people to have a good experience and buy from us again and if we communicate our genuine thanks for them being a customer they will notice.

Two, if we do it in the right way we can generate great social proof and the customer's communities will see them buying for our store.

So how do we set up a thank-you remarketing campaign?

You want to be doing this where recent customers can easily comment, so good platforms are Facebook, Instagram and Twitter.

Create three- to five-day remarketing lists based on visitors that have bought.

Set up adverts that thank the customer for their order and invite people to comment on the advert thread: i.e. 'Let us know about your experience on our website.'

Of course, you can control the comments, but you should get lots of social proof building on the advert which should help remove any buyer's remorse and aid them to buy more in the future.

We find that this advert sometimes has return on spend of over 20 times.

Why?

Why would people who have just bought, buy again?

Well, often this is one of the best times to sell more as customers are in the honeymoon phase and open to adding another item.

COMMUNICATE OFTEN

At university Mark used to live with six other lads.

It was the usual student chaos, but with an unusually tidy kitchen.

Quite often he would come into the kitchen and find it dirty and clean it. Do the dishes, sweep the floor, etc. Sometimes he would do a big clean.

Occasionally, they would argue about people not pulling their weight around the house and the finger would be pointed at Mark.

In his mind he found this unfair, but he realised that when he cleaned the kitchen or did any chores nobody was around to see it.

Consequently, he learnt to never clean the kitchen unless people were watching, or he made sure to tell people when they got home.

This simple lesson is apparent at running our agency business too. If ever we lose a client, often it's because we have been doing a lot of work behind the scenes and not communicating what we are doing. We feel like we are working hard, but the client is only experiencing a delay.

In fact, the projects where we go massively over budget and end up spending our own money are the very projects that clients get the most fed up with. Not only can the client not see the work, but they don't understand the complexity of the issues that have 'blown up the project.' We end up looking slow and stupid.

The solution is to script and automate regular communication to show that 'we are cleaning the kitchen and working very hard on it.' A clean kitchen is no good if the housemates have moved out waiting for it, i.e. customers leave.

For an e-commerce store the above is equally important. If you want to increase the likelihood of a customer buying again you need to communicate often, especially if there is a problem with the order. Someone may order an item and if you find it's out of stock or damaged, your team might be working hard to find a replacement, paying extra for delivery to get it there on time and working late to make sure it's dispatched. A whole lot of work, but unless the customer knows this they just experience a late order and are motivated to deliver a bad review which has knock-on effects.

With late orders and difficult deliveries we need to systemise personal communication points so that we communicate well. No customer is going to say, 'I ordered a present for my niece's wedding and the online store just kept emailing me and phoning me too many times to tell me it was going to be delivered on time.'

The trouble is when we get busy and the proverbial hits the fan, this is the exact time when we don't communicate. We hole up and get our heads down to get the job done. Thus, it's important to have a system that triggers the communication points when things go wrong so that customers get called, get emailed and understand what's happening. With any system you need a set of checks, to make sure that what you want to happen, happens.

USE PACING IN EMAILS

We have written and sent millions of email newsletters and learnt a few tricks of the trade.

Pacing was a huge win for us, and we have since learnt more about this from NLP, hypnosis and various sales trainings.

Pacing works everywhere. Just the other day Mark was looking for somewhere to sit in a lunch hall, and a person came up alongside him, matched his walking speed, walked with him and asked, 'Are you looking for somewhere to sit?' It was so in tune with what he was currently focusing on that he didn't even acknowledge that he didn't know this person.

Why do we want to use pacing?

Because once we pace a prospect, they are easier to lead to what action we want them to take.

Weather presenters use pacing; they always tell us what the weather is like today. That seems odd, doesn't it? We could just look out the window!

They tell us the current weather so that we can agree with them.

If we agree with them on the current weather, we are more likely to believe them when they make a prediction.

If we mention three things that are true, when we talk about a fourth it's more believable.

The best shop assistants don't ask the same dumb question to every person that walks in the store. Instead, they look to see what the person is doing and then ask them a question around that subject.

Shopper: Walks in and starts looking at camping stoves

Shop Assistant: 'Do you like cooking whilst camping? What camping food do you like?'

This is so much better than 'Can I help you today?'

For e-commerce emails we spend a lot of time researching where our buyer would be mentally when we send the email. What's in the news, how's the weather making them feel, what special events are on.

We build an email calendar with events and topics that are popular during that month. Our most successful campaigns have included:

- An offer for London Fashion Week for a discount clothing retailer. They had nothing to do with London Fashion Week but tying the email to something already in their mind due to the TV news worked.
- An offer for Father's Day where we told the recipient that their sons and daughters were not going to get them anything they actually wanted and so they may as well treat themselves.

If we tap into where the buyer is our emails have a much greater response.

How can we take it further?

Can we be like a weather presenter and tell them something that they know is true?

Yes, why not try these techniques:

- Dynamically add in a positive review they have written about a past purchase: i.e. Last time you shopped with us you bought *xyz* product, here's what you said about it '...' If they have scored the product purchase high and they see their own comments about how great it is, then it's much more likely that they will want to buy again.
- Personalise the email, not just the first name but other details like the country they live in, for example, 'How's the weather in <insert county> at the moment? Perhaps these offers might cheer you up.'
- Tell them the products that they already own and ask them to add to their wardrobe or collection.
- Show them what they recently looked at on the store.

If we bring personalised information about the recipient into the email that they can agree with AND combine it with what's already in their mind (Father's Day, Olympics, etc.), then we can pace with them and lead them to action.

GIVE YOUR CUSTOMERS SOMETHING TO TALK ABOUT

Dad always insisted that we had a sit-down dinner together. We think he thought it was important because he never had that with his parents.

As a fourth-generation baker, his parents were always too tired or working to have enough time to create a sit-down meal with everyone present.

Even though my father was a baker too, we had that sit-down meal.

We are glad we did, because we got a business education at that table every night.

My mum and dad ran several bakeries across Staffordshire and the evening meal became the forum to talk shop.

They would talk about the Alton Towers contract, the JCB deliveries, new product lines, staff issues, recipe ideas—we listened to everything.

It was a small business and the supermarkets were expanding rapidly and bakeries were shutting down everywhere.

But my parents' businesses thrived.

They had no marketing budget, no website and no sales team.

However, they did do marketing.

The marketing they did was all about empowering customers to become their sales team.

For example, we would listen to them talking about customer complaints and how they dealt with them. Instead of trying to get the person out the door as quickly as possible they made sure that the person who complained left with a smile on their face.

Why?

Because they knew that people talk about a business a lot more when something bad has happened to them. People love to vent and complain. So, they made sure that when someone came in and complained they left with a bunch of free cakes, a tour of the bakery and an amazing story to tell.

This way, the person could start the story with 'You know, I had a burnt cake from Hammersley's Bakery' but then the story would end with 'but they gave me four free pork pies and I went on a tour round the bakery and it was amazing, they really have a great setup there.'

Everyone loves free food, especially when it's delicious.

What they focused on with their marketing was giving customers interesting stories to tell about Hammersley's Bakery. Good stories travel, and they are the best type of marketing because it's free.

They also made sure that people who could talk the most, had the best stories to tell. These were the 'influencers' that could transform a business, the people that others would follow. Back then this was the town mayor, the head of 'The Round Table,' and local business leaders, and boy, did they love my dad's pies!

So, think about your own customers; what stories are you giving them to tell? Are you giving them enough of a narrative for them to say, 'You'll never guess what happened when I bought *X* from *Y* shop!'

So, add some surprise to their orders, something unexpected, something novel—and ultimately something that people will want to talk about.

A good example of how this kind of marketing can scale is Zappos.

Jeff Bezos (the owner of Amazon) got so worried about Zappos that he had to buy them.

The book *Delivering Happiness* by Tony Hsieh talks about the growth of the online shoe business Zappos.

The overall message is about customer service and going the extra mile. In fact, they have a name for it: 'random acts of WOWness.'

Over the years the number one driver of growth at Zappos has been repeat customers and word of mouth.

Their thinking has been to take most of the money they would have spent on advertising and spend it instead on customer service.

If the customer is wowed then they will talk about it to their friends and family.

It starts with their purchasing, delivery and return policies. They offer free shipping and free returns for starters; they also offer a 365-day return policy (how about that to make you sweat).

A lot of websites hide their phone number as they want people to order online, but at Zappos it's big and prominent on any page. (It's a big mistake to hide your phone number.)

Companies spend millions on social media doing brand building. However, that 10–15 minutes you have a customer's undivided attention on the phone is the biggest branding opportunity that you have.

Customers remember the phone call with your company for a long time.

The call centres should not be seen as a cost to minimise but instead as a key driver of lifetime customer value.

Some customers might call for their first order and then order online knowing they are dealing with a company that cares.

Zappos believes that lifetime customer value is a moving target and if they can increase the positive emotional connections with Zappos this metric will grow.

An example of Zappos' approach to increasing lifetime value is to give free upgrades to overnight shipping to the most loyal repeat customers.

Many call centres are measured by the KPI average handle time, which focuses on how many phone calls a person can make a day. This means that there is incentive to get customers off the phone as quickly as possible. Zappos does not measure call times and does not upsell on phone calls.

What's also crazy is that when a customer calls asking for some shoes that they don't have in stock the sales rep is trained to look for three competitors' websites that offer the product. So, they lose that sale but build rapport with the customer for the next purchase.

THINK OUTSIDE THE BOX

If we really want to grow our revenue, sometimes we have to think outside of the norm and to do this I'd like to introduce you to another classic marketing book.

There really are only four or five marketing books ever written that are worthy of being called a classic.

The Robert Collier Letter Book is one of them.

Written in 1931, you might ask what this book can help us with now. It's crazy to think that we can learn about selling on an e-commerce site from a man who lived in a totally different world.

But this is a book about one man's success at selling stuff via direct response letters. These are the letters that worked, and he explains why.

We think the genius of the book is his focus on the mechanism of the sale. A lot of the time his letters promised offers such as 'respond to this letter, get the product for 30 days and then pay only if you like it.'

If we break it down, for a sale to happen we need:

- The customer to choose to receive the product.
- The customer to choose the delivery method.
- The customer to pay for the product.
- The customer to decide to keep the product.

Each step for the customer has a different value. The amount of persuasion that needs to happen to move them to the desired outcome is also different for each step.

By moving the payment to after the person has tried the product or the service makes it much more likely that the customer proceeds with step 1.

This is hard to do if you are selling an expensive product but there are scenarios where this might be possible.

- When you are selling a product that is low value to produce but high value to the customer. This could be an education product or course. Or potentially some branded sunglasses that are extremely cheap to make but have a high price tag.
- If you are selling B2B and have existing customers that you want to extend credit to.
- Really good B2C customers that are big buyers for you and always pay.

This might blow your mind and you will quickly think that some people might not end up paying. Yes, that will be the case BUT what if the extra profit from this method more than paid for those people that did not end up paying?

This is counter intuitive because our fear of loss is strong. We often get so obsessed with those customers that might rob us that we don't care that we can double our profit per customer.

We are not saying this is the right method for all e-commerce sites, it's not, but I like to open up the assumptions around the business model because often lying here is a gold mine.

Moving onto point 2 above: 'The customer to choose the delivery method.' At first look this seems obvious but where there is a decision for the customer there are potentials for conversion rate gains.

How much you charge for the product and how much you charge for delivery will have a huge impact on the profitability per visitor.

You must choose how much to charge for delivery and how much to charge for the product.

We all have seen those free book offers on Facebook where you *just* must pay for shipping. Of course, the shipping cost covers the cost of the book too.

But in the mind of the buyer the focus is on the shipping.

The book is being offered free. There are also products being sold like this on Facebook: 'free ring, just pay shipping.'

The fact that these work means that we should experiment with how much we charge for the product and how much for shipping.

The above covers point 3, so this leaves 4: 'the customer to decide to keep the product.' This is a big one, especially in areas like women's clothing where returns can hit 40%!

What are you doing to reduce the returns rate? Probably very little.

But it's a huge area to work on. Post-purchase split tests on the following can have big dividends:

- Follow up with 50% of the customers with an email telling them how to use the product, a video on how to care for it, etc. Does this raise or lower the returns rate?
- Give 50% a free surprise gift with delivery. Does the gift pay for itself in the reduction of returns?
- Follow up with 50% with a personal email from the company director asking them specifically how they are getting on with the product. Does this increase or lower the returns rate?
- Follow up to 50% asking them to review the product before it has arrived. Ask the other 50% to review the product after it has arrived. How does the timing of the review affect returns?

What we are pointing out with all the above is that the sale is not a done deal. It's made up of various elements that value can be shifted from and to.

Also, you don't get paid until the customer decides to keep the product. We often have a fire and forget attitude to the order confirmation page.

In the words of Arnold Schwarzenegger, 'I'll be back,' is what we need the customers to say every time they buy.

WHAT IF CHARLIE MUNGER WANTED TO LOWER YOUR LIFETIME CUSTOMER VALUE?

Charlie Munger, Warren Buffett's partner, wrote a great book called *Poor Charlie's Almanack*.

It's a big book and totally fascinating to me.

It's certainly no novel and you must dive off into the other books he recommends to get a true idea of what he is talking about. But given he is one of the richest men in the world we would not expect to understand it first try.

One of his overriding themes is to study different disciplines widely and bring what works from one into another.

He also has a mantra which is 'invert, always invert.' By this he means turn a problem on its head. For example, if you were trying to work out which stocks to invest in, he might ask 'which stocks should we definitely not invest in' first.

In terms of e-commerce optimisation, inverting might be useful to answer to gain insight.

So if we want to 'decrease lifetime customer values' what would we do? Here are some suggestions:

- We would hide the information about delivery cost and delivery time down in the footer, making it hard for people find.
- We would move the basket icon to a different place compared to normal sites so that people must think to find it.
- Make the checkout hard to use on mobile.
- If customers are happy with the service, don't let them review the product so that other people don't find out how good the service is, otherwise they might buy too.
- Put out-of-stock products at the top of the category pages so that customers think the site is low on stock and leave.
- Make the site really slow to load.
- Only put one image of the product so that people cannot see detailed views. Keep it vague so they buy from someone else.
- When you send out a huge mailing to the email list, make sure the site falls over under the huge increase of traffic. If the site is down this will stop people buying—good!
- Let your SSL certificate expire so that when people try and buy they get a 'this website is not safe' warning—this will help put them off.
- Put all the Add to Basket and Proceed to Checkout buttons below the fold. This will sneakily hide them from buyers.
- When someone does manage to buy something, make sure you take a long time to deliver it and provide very little communication. Otherwise they might buy again—bad.
- If you sell products that other people sell, make sure your products are higher priced, offer no extra incentive to buy from you and have higher delivery costs. This one is a winner.
- Hire a dodgy SEO company and get banned from Google.

That was quite fun, and we could go on and on. However, the scary thing is that we have seen all the above happen and many are still quite common.

HOW TO RAISE THIS KPI— LIFETIME CUSTOMER VALUE

- Experiment with customer's first order—give 50% of customers a free gift or an upgrade in delivery. Calculate the event on repeat purchase rate—the goal is to find something you can add for X to receive $2X$ in LTCV value boost.
- Create a post-purchase thank-you campaign, i.e. remarket to customers who have just bought on Facebook with a thank-you post, thanking everyone for their order. These types of advert receive lots of comments and social proof which builds on the customers' loyalty to the brand.
- Implement a loyalty scheme and use points in marketing, points expiry emails, etc.—double points weekend.
- Offer upgrades to products already owned, i.e. offer buyers of a certain jacket a replacement jacket in the same size at a decent discount and phrase it as an upgrade.
- Use statistics to work out the link between customer review score and lifetime customer value. We often find that 4 / 5 reviewers buy significantly less than 5 / 5 reviewers—so have a system in place for 4 / 5 review customer orders to increase their experience with the brand.
- Implement buyer questions to involve buyers of certain products to respond to visitors' questions about the product they own. Asking them to answer questions often makes them state positively their experience anchoring the store with a quality experience.
- Create a premium buyers' club for top buyers, notice them and make a fuss of them, send them thank-yous, e.g. cinema vouchers if they clear a certain spend in 12 months.
- Follow up with purchasers three months after purchase in a non-sales email, just text from a person at customer services checking on how they are getting on with their product. Show you are invested in their experience long after the fact.
- Find your sweet spot for the second purchase, often it's sooner than you think—usually within 30 days; during this time the buyer is hyper responsive and you can send more marketing emails with a lower change of unsubscribe. Use this chance to get the second sale.

- Create a specific online series of videos on how to get the best out of *xyz* products. Choose the bestsellers and make sure that people have the best experience; map it out, for example, clothing video on 'How To Care For The Avalino Suit.'
- Ask customers to complete surveys and ask them to state what they like about the brand; this psychologically induces them to increase their preference for the brand—this is good to do to lapsed customers to reignite the memories or even rewrite them.
- Build a Facebook group for products' owners to meet and talk about the products, build a community.
- Uncover exactly what products people buy when they have the highest LTCV, push these products more in marketing knowing they have a good chance of building long-term customers.

RECAP:
LIFETIME CUSTOMER VALUE

Tracking lifetime customer value involves a number of different steps, including considering the type of customers you have, the coupons they use, their overall satisfaction and their delivery choices.

KPI: LIFETIME CUSTOMER VALUE—THE TOTAL REVENUE DIVIDED BY THE TOTAL NUMBER OF CUSTOMERS.

Put it to use:
- LTCV helps you track the products that lead to the highest lifetime value.
- Providing discount coupons, in the right setting, helps increase lifetime value.
- Use ScentTrail to track the type of customers you recruit and which products work best to recruit them.
- Upload customer email lists in Google AdWords so you can continually show your ad or products to customers on the list.
- Track this KPI regularly and watch it year after year to see how it changes.

Answer the following:

- What customers are you recruiting? Does your business naturally lead to high repeat purchase rates?
- What delivery options do your customers choose most often? What delivery rates do repeat customers opt for?
- Has your average review rating increased or decreased since your business began? This can tell you immediately whether your customers are happy with you and your products.
- How do you track the effect of marketing channels? After reading this chapter, what do you think the benefits of using ScentTrail to track LTCV marketing channels would be?
- Would you be willing to offer a lapsed customer a special rate if it meant increasing your LTCV overall? What type of special offer do you think would encourage a lapsed customer to come back to your website and make a purchase?

*See back of book for all of our recaps and step-by-step instructions for KPIs all in one handy workbook.

GROWTH OF SIX-MONTH CUSTOMER RECRUITMENT YEAR ON YEAR

This is the total number of customers recruited for the past six months compared to the same figure at this point for the prior year. This reveals the best metrics to predict whether growth will continue. This figure has to be tracked, as it is not available in Google Analytics. It's one of the things we realised was a valuable figure to look at, and you can work it out in Excel using your real customer data. If the total number of customers stopped growing, it becomes like a headwind, or more like a wall. It's harder to achieve other KPIs and succeed with them when the number of customers continues to decline year on year.

For this KPI, we look at year-on-year results because if you notice the number is declining year on year, it means you have less growth than you've had before. We check this number in six-month blocks, because looking at one month at a time won't provide a true picture of what's happening. You cannot look at recruitment in December and compare it to the other months of the year as you will be getting vastly different recruitment figures in December due to seasonality. Averaging out over six months, using the running total for each month and comparing it to where you were last year at the same time, gives you an important look into your customer recruitment rate.

For instance, let's say you wanted to see if you've experienced any growth between August and December of 2016. You'd compare the number of customers recruited during those months to the same time (August to December) in 2015.

If you're growing, and your customer recruitment rate is staying the same, you're probably going to be okay, as long as your customer rate doesn't go down. However, most businesses want to increase their recruitment rate. If you understand the amount you want to increase your recruitment rate, that will help you build a model for where you want to be in six months or in a year. Because of this, the six-month recruitment rate is one of the key figures that lets us know if growth is working well.

When you compare a recent recruitment rate to a previous one, look and see if the rate is dropping; this should be a warning sign. You're going to have a much harder time growing your business, even with the other KPIs. Some KPIs, specifically those that deal with conversion, directly affect your customer recruitment rate. As these KPIs increase, increasing the customer recruitment rate becomes easier. Bottom line: you have to make sure all your channels are working to deliver customers to you.

If your customer recruitment rate is dipping, some questions to ask include:
- What trackable things have you done to contribute to this? Have you

changed your recruitment offer? Have you reduced your AdWords spend? Are you not recruiting as many customers on social media?

• How are your other marketing channels performing? If they are not delivering customers to you, figure out which channels are not recruiting as they did the previous year, then dive in and tweak what is wrong.

The customer recruitment rate year on year is a good way to measure your business's progress and growth. It can help you recognise early warning signs, so adjustments can be made.

THINK IN TERMS OF E-COMMERCE SALES FUNNELS

To recruit new customers you need a new customer recruitment sales funnel. To introduce this idea quickly to you let me show you one client's marketing funnel.

Platform	Campaign	Campaign Type	Budget %	Traffic type Funnel
Google	DoubleClick	Display	10.00%	Freezing
Facebook	Reach & Frequency	Display	10.00%	Freezing
Facebook	Demographic Profile	Conversion	3.00%	Cold
Google	Car Parts	Search	6.00%	Cold
Google	Tier 1	Shopping	3.00%	Cold
Google	Tier 2	Shopping	5.00%	Warm
Google	Tier 3	Shopping	8.00%	Warm
Google	RLSA	Search	10.00%	Warm
Affiliate			5.00%	Warm
Google	Shopping RLSA	Shopping	10.00%	Warm
Google	Brand	Search	3.00%	Warmer
Google	Brand	Shopping	3.00%	Warmer
Facebook	Gen Web Visitors	Dynamic Product Remarketing	12.00%	Warmer
Google	Brand RLSA	Search	3.00%	Hot
Google	Brand Discount	Search	3.00%	Hot
Facebook	ATB	Dynamic Product Remarketing	6.00%	Hot

On the right you can see how 'hot' this marketing is. By hot we mean how close to making a sale the marketing activity is. But we start with freezing, because we know that if we don't fill the funnel in the top, then nothing will come out the bottom.

You start with the hot layers first and then build out. Once you get this all working together an e-commerce site hits its tipping point.

Malcolm Gladwell talks about that moment when EVERYTHING HAPPENS in his book *The Tipping Point*.

With our online stores this happens with our marketing campaigns. That's hard for a beginner to get their head around because they might spend x amount on Facebook or AdWords and get nothing and so stop.

Facebook is particularly prone to the tipping point. This is because when you start a campaign your advert has no social interaction, therefore no social proof, and people write you off. Spend another chunk of money on the ad and suddenly you have likes, shares and comments that show you are the real deal.

Our more simple funnels involve flushing out the potential buyers with Google Shopping and then remarketing to them based on site behaviour with carefully selected ads on social media and email.

These remarketing ads tend to only work once they have social proof, comments and shares.

The simple one-two-three punch works like this:

1. Get people who are interested in buying x product to put their hand up on Google Shopping/AdWords.
2. Remarket to the people that didn't buy (Facebook, GDN, e-mail) with content that shows that:
    »   People love this product, e.g. good reviews, lots of likes, shares and comments.
    »   Lots of people buy it, e.g. images of products in actual buyer homes.
    »   This brand delivers, e.g. good third-party reviews for shipping and experience.
3. Post-purchase follow-up to make sure these buyers buy again as quickly as possible.

The trigger point for the whole sequence comes when point 2 is working and triggered.

That's the essential step that moves your offer above the competition.

Most e-commerce store marketing we see do point 1 and then have a tick-in-the-box point 2 strategy that never triggers. So, results are poor.

(NB. Regarding point 3, we very rarely see this done well at all. With one of our biggest customers we spent ages working out the exact amount of free loyalty points to give with each first-time order to receive the most repeat purchases in the next 30 days.)

HOW TO RAISE THIS KPI—SIX-MONTH CUSTOMER RECRUITMENT

- Create a split testing program for key landing pages, use a tool like unbounce to quickly iterate to higher converting offers and imagery.
- Close the revenue attribution loop, i.e. if phone calls are a decent proportion of revenue use a tool like Response Tap to match phone order value to marketing spend. Only when you understand the full value of all marketing can you work out where to spend more.
- Use split testing to work on your key SEO pages. Google measures rank factors such as bounce rate. Therefore, highlight the SEO landing pages and split test them in a tool like Optimisely just for natural search traffic. Work out which images get the lowest bounce rate, what fonts, what layout, etc. These can be blog pages or product pages, but make sure your SEO landing pages have high engagement and Google will send you more traffic and often natural SEO traffic is new customers.
- Work out the weakest times of the year for recruitment; what can you do to reduce the impact? Can you move the sale earlier or later, what do you need to do to keep recruitment high when attention is lower?
- Try using social proof on product pages, such as 'James from Manchester just bought the Avalino Suit' or 'Low Stock Item and Five People Viewing This Right Now.'
- Be dynamic with your offers; many of the big UK sites like BooHoo have a dedicated offer team that change the offer throughout the day based on how sales are going. If demand is high they reduce the offer, if sales are not going so well they roll out better offers to hit the target. They react in real time to the market conditions with variable delivery rate, etc.
- Use countdown times with real offers that run out to create urgency.
- Have a reason why on your offers, psychologically having a reason why you are having a sale makes it much more successful, for example, 10 Year Birthday—London Fashion Week offer—try and tie it to what the consumer is already thinking about.
- Don't use tick-in-the-box remarketing; instead, work out your 'remarketing stack.' Work out the critical sales cycle using Google Analytics, e.g. three days or seven days, and then tailor your remarketing

so that the prospects get different messages each day. Day 1—key objection number 1—social proof, Day 2—key objection number 2—returns information, etc., and mirror this across all remarketing channels—Facebook, Google, etc.

- Identify new customers on the site and give them different offers than existing customers. Understand their history on the site.

- Make it very easy for repeat visitors to find what they were looking for last time on the site; put 'recently viewed products' right in their path in the main navigation.

- Make sure the basket is persistent and it's still there when they come back on the same or different device.

- Sculpt your affiliate scheme to reward customer recruitment above all else, pay more for new customers and work with affiliates that can drive new customers to the site, give them more incentive and sales thresholds so they feature you more in their emails. Make sure your affiliate scheme has the best statistics on Affiliate Window (or equivalent) for your market so you become the obvious choice to push.

- Optimise your Google Shopping product feed for traffic; it's not a done-once-and-forget activity.

- Use a tool like Mouseflow to watch new visitors on the site; what do they struggle with, how do they navigate? Tag them so you can separate them from existing customers as these guys already know how to use the site. Optimise for the new visitors to make it easier for them to get started.

- Create engagement devices on the home page with a tool like 'lead quizzes' to increase engagement and to allow them to find what they need quickly.

- Make sure the site can handle Black Friday email sendouts without falling over!

- Positioning—sometimes less is more; try removing low click through products in categories to see if they are lowering the brand value in the new visitors' eyes.

RECAP: GROWTH OF SIX-MONTH CUSTOMER RECRUITMENT YEAR ON YEAR

Your recruitment rate should stay the same or increase year on year. If you compare the last six months to the same time last year and the rate is lower, there is a definite issue. Sometimes it's another KPI. Other KPIs that affect conversion rates can affect your recruitment rate. Fixing these other indicators will usually help increase this KPI.

KPI: GROWTH OF SIX-MONTH CUSTOMER RECRUITMENT YEAR ON YEAR

This refers to the total number of customers you have recruited in the last six months. Add these together, then compare them to the same data gathered the prior year.

Put it to use:
- This KPI helps you determine if your business will continue to grow.
- Cannot be found in Google Analytics, but may be worked out in Excel.
- If this number declines, it means you're experiencing less growth. This is a warning sign.
- Some KPIs will affect your recruitment rate. If they aren't doing well, your recruitment rate will show it.

Answer the following:
- Use an Excel sheet to calculate your current six-month recruitment rate. What is it? Compare it to the previous year's. Did the amount increase, decrease or stay the same?
- If the number decreased, look at the other KPIs. Are they functioning as they should be? If not, what steps will you take to resolve this issue?
- Consider other trackable things you've done to contribute to a lower recruitment number. Write them here and check each one.
- What marketing channels do you use? How are they performing?

- What steps can you take next to increase your six-month customer recruitment rate year on year?

*See back of book for all of our recaps and step-by-step instructions for KPIs all in one handy workbook.

AVERAGE ORDER VALUE ROBUSTNESS

The average order value is compared year on year. This is available in Google Analytics but what's key here is the ability to grow traffic while keeping or increasing the average order value. As you add traffic and spend more in channels like Google AdWords, the law of diminishing returns means that incremental traffic is going to be more expensive as you bid on more generic terms. You cannot afford to do this if as traffic grows the average order value declines. It's simple math, but extremely vital.

If your AOV is too low, then it will act like a noose around your e-commerce store, stifling growth. If you have a low AOV, you need an increased amount of lifetime customer value, otherwise you simply cannot grow.

So ideally you need one of the following scenarios:

- High AOV and 1.5x purchase frequency a year.
- Low AOV and 5x purchase frequency a year.

Also consider your margin. If your AOV is low, such as an AOV under £50, then your margin is going to be tighter. This means you have to be very careful with your cost per acquisition. AOV and LTCV are very significant if you want scalable growth.

Fundamentally AOV is important to your website, because this KPI is another way to give yourself an immediate increase in revenue. As you increase traffic and conversion rate, there's no point in increasing the add-to-basket rate or checkout-to-order rate if your AOV value is too low. Even if you're experiencing more sales at a lower value, this still might mean less revenue. As you increase the traffic to your website, you want to see your AOV being robust. As your AOV reduces, it also does the following:

- Reduces lifetime customer value.
- Reduces overall revenue.
- Reduces cost per acquisition needed on channels like Google AdWords making you need a much higher conversion rate than your competitors.

Basket Size & AOV

So, how do you increase the average order value?

- Allow bundles.
- Increase the use of machine learning to understand what products are bought often with other products to make purchases easier.
- Improve navigation to make it easier for customers to move around your website.
- Find one-click upsells for the basket pages that are a no-brainer. Like 'add a belt for £5 to the pair of trousers in your basket.'
- Improve the look and features of your website.
- Frequently bought together functionality.
- Post-purchase upsells through the use of payment methods such as Stripe.

A key way to increase the AOV is to understand and increase the number of items that customers add to basket. There are two ways of increasing your basket size. It's pretty simple: you either increase the number of items in the basket, or increase the prices. Plugins and extensions can help you with either of these options with simple systems and widgets.

If you want to increase the AOV significantly, like by 50%, the best option is to increase your basket value. You can increase your price slightly and maintain your customer base, but you'll fundamentally change your entire shop if you attempt to achieve a 50% higher AOV by raising your prices. Customers are not likely to purchase something for £200 they could have paid £100 for yesterday. You have to be careful as the AOV can be a fundamental part of your value proposition, so changes can (and should be) done slowly. A good target would be to increase AOV by 10% year on year.

For higher AOV, increasing the basket size is the best bet. The best way to increase the AOV is to increase the perceived value and ease of buying more. You could try doing an Amazon Prime-style approach offering next-day delivery for a year in return for a small fee. We've seen this increase conversion in all cases.

For example:

Example of AOV boosts

- Hanna instruments product and basket
- Div add to basket popup

On this image, a simple system shows items that are frequently purchased with the item your customer has already added to their basket. This system can be manually populated by you or can be created automatically on your site. Obviously, an automated system is always best.

You can also create bundled promotions and slight discounts for additional items. These are very easy to implement and if you don't offer bundles, we always say it's like leaving money on the table.

Just think, you've already done the hard work. You got their attention, you've led them to your site, they've added items to their cart and believe in your store and your product enough to complete the purchase. Why wouldn't you offer additional add-to-basket items for a quick extra sale? If you ignore this one feature, you're going to lose a lot of revenue annually.

HOW TO RAISE THIS KPI— AVERAGE ORDER ROBUSTNESS

It's important to increase the average order value while scaling traffic. There is no point doubling traffic and halving the AOV, as this would put you in exactly the same place revenue wise.

So here are some of the ways we have moved this KPI north:

- Making it easier to buy more will always help; one way to do this is to move to a payment method like Stripe which can save credit card details for a short period of time. This allows you to get the transaction in the bag before offering a one-click upsell. Traditionally you would have had to offer the upsell prior to the checkout thus increasing friction before the checkout. Now you can offer a post-purchase upsell with no downside.

- Use machine learning to offer related products and set the metrics to increase return on visitor. The amount of data machine learning can use will mean over time it will beat your manual suggestions.

- Make your site super fast. Buyers will allocate subconsciously x amount of time for their purchase. If the site is super fast then they will look around for other items and add more to the basket. If the site is slow then they will buy only the essentials and sometimes give up entirely.

- Use social proof to show that 'most people buying this tend to also buy this' as a suggestion to help people buy more.

- Spot common paths throughout the site and put them onto the add-to-basket pop-up, i.e. if people buying x product tend to go back to y category after adding an item then show that as an option on the pop-up. Or if they tend to check out after they have added four items point them in the direction of the checkout.

- Optimise category listings for revenue per visitor, rather than bestseller order. This will push products that overall produce the highest value for their view, rather than just getting an order regardless of the size.

- Split test the free shipping threshold and optimise for revenue; you will find a sweet spot that is often different from the guess that you started out with.

- Offer discounts that increase with the basket value. Tell people how much they could save by adding x amount. See vendors like Beaverbrooks who do this well with their jewellery, i.e. spend £50 and get £25 of free jewellery—then when the buyer has £75 in their basket tell them 'if you added £25 of jewellery to your basket you would get £50 worth of free jewellery'—then when they have £150 worth of jewellery in their basket tell them 'add £50 worth of jewellery and you would get £100 of free jewellery' and so on.

- Create 'get the look' bundles so that people can add many items that go together to the basket all in one go.
- Offer a gift card to increase average order value. If you have a free delivery threshold you could offer buyers the option of topping up their purchase to the threshold with a gift card. This means they get free delivery and can use the gift card on the next purchase.
- Show order increasing offers with countdown timers to increase scarcity so people act sooner rather than later.
- Use the reward scheme to increase order value by offering double points over a certain purchase threshold.
- Offer a free product as an incentive if they spend over a certain amount.
- High price anchoring—split a very high priced product alongside your bestsellers. This high priced item won't sell that often but will make the other products look much better value as the visitors will be anchored to the higher price.
- Use personalisation when existing customers visit the store. You know what they already own and you can offer much better suggestions based on their previous purchases. You can even offer them upgrades on their past purchases, for example, an extra pair of trousers for the suit they bought on a previous visit.
- Offer finance to make it easy to spread payment. In Australia a service like Afterpay works really well by not charging the buyer any more and splitting the payment into five payments.

RECAP: AVERAGE ORDER VALUE ROBUSTNESS

While perhaps not the first KPI you look at, the average order value is probably the most important of all seven. If this value is too low, your add-to-basket rate or checkout-to-order rate cannot grow. It also affects your lifetime customer value, revenue and marketing costs.

KPI: AVERAGE ORDER VALUE ROBUSTNESS

The average, compared year on year, of the average value of orders and traffic growth.

Put it to use:
- You should always keep an eye on your average order value, as it can stifle or improve growth, depending on whether it is low or high.
- You should have a high AOV and 1.5x purchase frequency per year or a low AOV and 5x purchase frequency per year.
- As you increase the amount of traffic and the conversion rate of your website, your AOV should increase as well.
- If your AOV isn't robust enough, it can negatively affect other KPIs.
- Increasing the customer's basket size or checkout amount can improve AOV.

Answer the following:
- What is your average order value? Is it high or low compared to the traffic rate and conversion rate you have?
- What are three products on your website that are frequently purchased together?
- What are three ways you can increase your average order value?
- Do you normally offer bundles? Do you think your customers would be open to purchasing more from you if they got a bundled promotion at a slight discount? Why or why not?

*See back of book for all of our recaps and step-by-step instructions for KPIs all in one handy workbook.

TRAFFIC GROWTH

TRAFFIC GROWTH

You cannot get around the fact that sites that consistently grow do increase their traffic over time. However, growing traffic can be expensive. First, you'll need to increase other KPIs like 'add-to-basket rate' and 'lifetime customer value.' Then you'll be able to afford to pay more for traffic than you could previously. This opens up traffic resources to you and allows you to scale. If your other KPIs are not in shape, then you simply cannot afford the costs of the traffic as your costs per acquisition will be too prohibitive.

Quite simply the competitor that can pay the most for the customer wins. To do this you need to have the highest converting store with the highest average order value. If you can pay more than your competitors for the same customer and still make the same amount of profit, then you are ultimately going to win the race.

One way to increase traffic is to increase SEO traffic. We know we said SEO was dead earlier, but it was only dead in its previous form—done well with a good content marketing strategy and great e-commerce structural SEO and you can still get good natural traffic from Google . However, an e-commerce setup implemented badly can be very slow and slow sites hurt SEO.

SPEED AND SEO

How your website operates can definitely affect your bottom line. For one of our clients, an increase in speed of 25% led to a 10% increase in conversion, or about £1 million additional revenue each year. Speed offers a great increase on investment. It took a few weeks of planning and coding, but the result was well worth it.

Speed

- 25% increase in speed led to a 10% increase in conversion, and increased natural ranking
- This led to circa £1million increase in revenue per year.

Speed tests, like YSlow or Google Page Speed, can help you keep track of the loading speed of your site, but some are better than others. Google Analytics, for instance, can test the speed of your website, but may not provide you with an accurate answer every time. This is because Analytics often confuses tracking code on your website and page load times. So, if you're trying everything possible to speed up your website, but Google is still saying that it's running slow, it may not be true. Google Analytics may simply not see the load times.

E-commerce SEO is a continual process, but there are two important things you need to consider when it comes to e-commerce and SEO:

You need the basic structure set up properly, which many sites have not, and, if you're migrating from one platform to another platform, the most important thing is to do so carefully and get expert advice if possible.

It's vital to figure out if you have any bad practices in place on your current website before moving everything over so you're not just repeating mistakes and continuing bad SEO. Often, we find developers change site URLs from one site to the new site just to make it easier for themselves, when this can cause a lot of issues. Sites should be built with a growth-first approach, rather than a development team first approach.

SEO

Our SEO Methodology Considerations – (This is a Continual Process)

1. Overall Configuration requirements
2. Canonical Tag Management
3. Product tag Conventions
4. Headings (H1, H2) Management
5. Product URLs
6. Layered / Faceted Navigation Issues.
7. Prevent search engines from accessing certain page – using custom robots file, no follows
8. Parameter Handling in Google Webmaster Tools
9. How to deal correctly with catalogue search pages.
10. Sitemaps (one for products and one for categories)
11. Hierarchical URLs (including category path within URLs)
12. Secure Pages and best practices
13. Pagination Structure.
14. Session IDs / SIDs
15. Speed
16. Proper Structure around 301 Setup and Management
17. Internal / Multiple Stores Environments and SEO essentials
18. Feed related issues with duplicate content

PAID TRAFFIC

Traffic growth is all about paid traffic. To make paid traffic work you need to be able to pay for the traffic and then make a profit after all costs are taken into consideration.

It's a numbers game and as you scale you will need to keep tweaking your optimisations to keep the profit window open.

Fundamentally this is the industry of advertising.

If you have not read *Scientific Advertising* by Claude Hopkins, it's my pleasure to introduce you to this book. Written in 1923 you'd wonder what relevance it has today for e-commerce but given the man's genius for marketing its learnings are evergreen.

Here is what David Ogilvy said of the book:

'Nobody should be allowed to have anything to do with advertising until he has read this book seven times. It changed the course of my life.'

Here are some key points that we can apply to our online stores that we can use to help scale our advertising spend profitably.

FAMILIARITY

If people are familiar with your brand, product and service before they decide they need *xyz* product they will more likely buy from you. Today brand awareness does not mean carpet bombing TV with generic adverts to hit everyone; instead, we can create a very specific audience and be totally focused on that audience. You need your store to be famous, but only with a tight subset of people. This is very possible with Facebook, Twitter, Google and LinkedIn.

So, the hard work comes down to really building up that audience list that you need to target knowing they are right in your sweet spot.

RUN THE NUMBERS

If Claude Hopkins found that he could send out 1000 coupons and get $5000 back, he would then send out 10,000 coupons and see if he could get $50,000 back. He would keep going until he couldn't find any more people to send coupons too. He went BIG and fast. With our e-commerce stores, as we have talked about before, we seem to have an internal thermostat that stops us spending more. We mentally tell ourselves 'we are not the type of business that spends £50K a month on Facebook' even though we would get a good return. If the numbers work, go big or go home.

PEOPLE LIKE CERTAINTY

Claude had early success with a restorative cure by making the pharmacist sign the guarantee about the product rather than the guarantee just being mentioned on the bottle. Guarantees are good but only if people trust the person offering the guarantee. With e-commerce we need to tie the guarantee back to a visible, real person that people trust. Making a guarantee from a faceless brand is much less powerful. Build some rapport with the store brand and a person who works there and then offer a personal guarantee.

PERSONALISATION

Personalisation might be the latest buzz word in e-commerce but back in 1929 Claude Hopkins already understood it. Selling life insurance to businessmen, a message was sent with the offer of a free book: 'Your name will be printed in gilt on each book'—the personalisation of the book with their name was novel at the time and it sold well.

We can use personalisation to match the product to the consumer. We can show the consumer their name embroidered on the suit inside pocket on the product page. We know their name, we know the product they are looking at and the technology is there to visualise the product with their name. Suddenly the product becomes much more personal to them.

HOW TO RAISE THIS KPI—TRAFFIC GROWTH

This KPI is constrained by all the other KPIs given that average order value, add to basket and basket to order percentage dictate how much traffic you can buy profitably. Of course if you could get traffic for free then your mission would be complete but most of the time you can't. The above said, there is still a lot you can do to increase traffic

Firstly SEO:

- A good content strategy is essential for SEO traffic. Start by answering the questions that people ask on Google surrounding your product. You can find what questions people have in the search query history of your AdWords account. Another good place is to look at the query report in Google Webmaster Tools, as this shows the search queries you appeared on but didn't actually get clicks. Use the filter to look for why, what, when, how, and you are bound to come up with a few gems.

- Use a tool like AHREFs to find the most popular and shared content in your niche; use this to get ideas for content.

- Find the top bloggers in your market who rank well for search terms you would like to do well on. Then scan their site with Screaming Frog to find their external links; spot the kind of content these influencers like to link to. Then create content they are more likely to link to on their site.

- Also scan the top bloggers' external links to find content that has been removed, recreate the resource on your own site and then notify the blogger; they might link to you instead.

- Create glossaries of terms used in your niche so that people find it on your site and share it.

- Scan the site with Screaming Frog to check for:
  - » Broken internal links.
  - » Excessive internal redirects to fix.
  - » Pages missing H1 and H2 titles.
  - » Pages missing titles.
  - » Images missing alt tags.
  - » Issues with your robots file.
  - » Googlebot loops from incorrect internal links.

- Make your site load as per Google Analytics under four seconds on average. Google likes fast sites.

- Use AHREFS to find your top content. These are your 'power pages'; use these pages to link to other pages that you want to rank better. Pick pages that you want to move up that are at the bottom page one on the search results.

- Pay particular attention to the title tag on the home page and the use of keywords on the main page titles of your site. A tweak here can usually do wonders.

ADWORDS

AdWords is one of the biggest areas to grow traffic and a good AdWords and Google Shopping strategy is a must. We are only going to mention a few things here as there is a whole other book we have written just on this subject.

- Make sure there are no errors or warnings in the Google Merchant centre for your feed. Even warnings affect the amount of clicks you get considerably.
- Use all the ad extensions available to allow Google's artificial intelligence to build an advert that works well. Price extensions, review extensions, callouts, sitelinks—the whole bundle.
- Pay particular attention to search queries every day and go through each one. Yes, it's a lot of work but it will give you an edge over the set and forget competition.
- Optimise your product feed; most merchants don't and it's a competitive advantage.
- Get a Google rep as they can opt you into betas and other experiments that can prove very lucrative. They can also see dashboard stats on your account that you cannot see.
- Try split testing with the different bidding models. Google's AWE is getting better each month—you probably won't be able to beat the machine soon.
- Pull off your competitors' keywords and best ads; don't start writing yours from scratch, stand on the shoulders of giants.
- Look at the best campaigns for your products in other countries—USA, Australia, UK, etc. Look for great advertising copy that you can use in your own adverts.
- Use AdWords scripting to check everything from landing pages, site links, price extensions to anomalies in the account.
- Make sure your agency reports weekly on your results, not monthly. Monthly is too late if something is wrong.

- Use a tool to take a screenshot of the first page of Google on your biggest search terms to watch how the offers change over time.
- Use a tool to take a screenshot of your competitors' home pages so you can see when their offers go live and which offers they repeat and don't repeat.

SOCIAL MEDIA MARKETING

Again, this is a subject larger than this book but let's talk about the bare essentials that work well for e-commerce on social media, with a focus on Facebook.

- Facebook remarketing is a must-do activity but don't just do this as a tick-in-the-box strategy. First look at how long your sales cycle is—from one day for car parts to a couple of weeks for men's clothes. This sales cycle length will dictate how compressed your remarketing stack needs to be. If your sales cycle is one week then your Facebook remarketing stack could look like this:
  » Day 1—remarket to people with audiences focusing on a) product viewers, b) add to baskets, and c) checkout abandoners—one day after the visit. Remarket to these audiences with a social proof campaign. To set up a social proof campaign create a post on your Facebook page which asks recent buyers to comment on their experience on the brand. Get good comments on this thread by retargeting recent buyers. You can edit and delete any negative comments. Then once you have a decent swarm of user-generated love for the brand in terms of comments, use this post to remarket to the *a*, *b*, and *c* audiences of new visitor traffic above. This will serve to show social proof for the brand.
  » Day 2—use dynamic remarketing to show the product they looked at on the site, preferably with a favourable review of the product from a recent buyer underneath.
  » Day 3—if they have not bought try a special offer here with a time pressure element.
  » Day 4—use a message campaign to ask for any questions they have

about buying the product they were looking for. Make it easy for them to reach out and start a conversation and buy.

- Facebook marketing to cold traffic. Upload your recent buyers to Facebook and then recreate a lookalike audience. Make sure you use the advanced setup where it splits the lookalike list into 1%, 2% and 3%–5% lists. You can set up campaigns for each % audience and test the ROI. Try catalogue ads with an offer. See which of the lookalike audiences gives you the best ROI. If you don't have many sales let Facebook optimise for a custom conversion that focuses on add-to baskets.

The main power that social media has is to add social proof to your brand. So you want to be thinking about how you can focus social proof into a certain set of posts and then how you can leverage this social proof to show new visitors that there is a buzz associated with your brand. Often we see the social proof is there but spread too thinly across all social activity and therefore quick glances from new visitors leave them unconvinced.

EMAIL

A lot more traffic can be driven from automated marketing surrounding visitor behaviour on the store. Here are some of the emails we use that have driven increasing sales.

- Abandoned cart emails—pretty standard these days, but the mistake people make is not split testing these emails. Also, if the customer is an existing customer tying these in with reward points can work well.
- Abandoned basket email—these are less well used as you need something to tie the session of the user to the email address as the email won't have been typed in yet at the basket stage.
- Abandoned product emails.
- Abandoned category emails.
- Abandoned home page emails.

To increase the email addresses that these behavioural emails can capture you need to:

- Encrypt the email address of the user in the newsletter click through URLs so the website can tie an email to a browser session.
- Use personalised banners and overlays on the site to capture emails

addressing in return for offer coupons. You only want to do this for users that you don't yet have an email for.

We have automated the above emails and email capture with our Bright Owl and ScentTrail systems.

Another general rule for email is send more email as people who unsubscribe are generally those that don't ever buy anyway. Also, when a buyer has just bought they are in a honeymoon period with brand and will accept a higher volume of emails than someone who has bought more than six months ago.

AFFILIATE MARKETING

Having worked with Affiliate Window for many years it amazes me how many people totally mess this channel up. Done badly this can end up clipping the ticket on orders that would have happened anyway. Done correctly and you can have a legion of commission-only salesmen promoting your brand. Here are our quick tips on getting this channel right.

- Only pay out commission on new customer orders, or at the very least pay more commission for customer recruitment.
- Don't pay commission on coupon codes that have not specifically been given to affiliates as affiliate codes.
- Watch your stats, make sure that your validation rate and other stats are better than your competitors' on the platform; you want to be the obvious choice to promote for the big affiliates.
- Work with an experienced affiliate manager (yes, like us) who has relationships with all the top affiliate sites. It takes years to get to know who is who in these companies and to befriend them at networking events. What's more, we can ring them up and talk to them about 10 brands at once. They don't have time to talk to individual brands unless they are a High Street name. A good affiliate manager will also know how to get you placed on sites like MoneySavingExpert and Hot UK Deals.
- Bug Affiliate Window more; left alone, they will do nothing for the override and fee, and it's a lot about 'he who shouts loudest' that gets attention.
- Make sure your product feed works and is error free.

- Keep your banners updated and regularly send useful information to your top affiliates.
- Cut back on affiliates that send a lot of traffic but no or few sales. For example, competition sites will send a lot of traffic but no sales. These will affect your affiliate conversion rate, making your program look poor.

RECAP: TRAFFIC GROWTH

To increase the amount of traffic to your online store, you need to be able to pay more for a customer than your competitor can. This means making sure all of your KPIs, especially lifetime customer value and add to basket, are improved so your traffic resources are available and you are able to increase your traffic numbers.

KPI: Traffic Growth—Put it to use:
- Increase traffic with SEO. With a great marketing strategy and e-commerce structural SEO, you can achieve natural traffic through Google.
- Make sure the e-commerce structure is correct or it can lead to bad SEO.
- The way your website operates affects revenue and traffic growth. Slow sites kill traffic.
- Use Google Page Speed or YSlow for page speed times. Google Analytics tends to get confused.

Answer the following:
- How well are your other KPIs performing? Can you afford to move your attention to this KPI or do you need to spend more time on the add-to-basket KPI or LTCV KPI first?
- Is your e-commerce site implemented correctly? If you can't answer this question, or you can't say yes for certain, get the help of a professional. A poor structure leads to poor results.
- How often do you test the speed of your website? What speed tests do you use? What is your average load time?

*See back of book for all of our recaps and step-by-step instructions for KPIs all in one handy workbook.

BASKET-TO-ORDER RATE

Basket-to-order rate is the orders divided by the people that add an item to the basket. Typically, we split this down into basket to checkout and checkout to order, but sometimes there is so much funky stuff such as PayPal Express going on at the basket it's good to have an overall number. This is a great metric to improve and many sites want to jump to this straight away. However, we usually find we can get more revenue from improving the add-to-basket rate first and then optimising the higher numbers of shoppers later that this provides.

GETTING VISITORS TO PROCEED TO CHECKOUT

Remember, according to our statistics, an average of 55% of the people who have added something to their basket will click Proceed to Check Out. While this may seem like a low percentage, there are several reasons that people abandon ship at this point in time.

COUPON CODES AND PAYPAL EXPRESS

With one of our clients, for instance, the issue was occurring in the coupon code section of the basket page. After discovering this, we had the system e-mail us immediately each time there was a failed coupon. Most of the coupon codes entered that were considered duds had only one digit wrong. Because they didn't work, however, the customer abandoned his basket and left the website. This resulted in a lot of lost revenue for our client. To solve this, we made the decision, with the client, to apply the discount automatically. This way, even if the client accidentally got the coupon code wrong, he would still receive the discount and proceed to checkout. This one change alone makes the client over £1 million every year.

Basket - Coupon Usability

- What happens if a users enters a dud code
  - Do you log it
  - Do you want to show them a valid offer
  - How can you handle it better – what would a good physical sales assistant do?

Another roadblock that may be discouraging customers from clicking proceed to checkout is actually PayPal Express. We found that this is beneficial when it comes to new customers, but not so much when it comes to recurring customers. After researching this phenomenon, we've determined that new customers enjoy using Paypal Express because it's a safer way for them to pay for your products. They don't quite trust you yet, so safety is key for them. Test it to see how it works for you.

To encourage customers to proceed to the next step, or purchase the items, make sure the basket clearly shows exactly what the product will cost them, and how long delivery is going to be and how much. Also make the payment icons really prominent on the basket page. Companies like Visa and Mastercard spend millions of dollars annually to associate their logos with trust. Leverage this marketing to increase the basket-to-order KPI. This takes away a lot of anxiety your customers may have about their purchase.

The browser abandonment pop-ups can be very useful here as well. If a customer starts to exit the page, a pop-up offering them an additional 10% off might just sway them to stay. Just make sure the pop-ups are timed perfectly to catch a buyer's attention.

GETTING VISITORS FROM CHECKOUT TO ORDER CONFIRMATION

Approximately 84% of visitors go from checkout to order confirmation. Most individuals with e-commerce sites worry about this part of the process, mainly because it's easy to see what the consequences (the lost revenue) are. As soon as you put your events into Google Analytics, you can see the amount of money, to the penny, you're losing.

That can be scary because seeing these numbers, you may say, 'Hey, wait a minute, we just lost twenty thousand pounds over the past month from one step of the checkout process to the next!'

The reality is, you're going to lose some of your customers at this step, but this is also the area where you can get the best win if you've established your value proposition right, have a competitive product, are selling at the right price, have your site merchandised properly and have your delivery terms sorted out. People are more likely to put up with a checkout process that doesn't work that well or is slightly confusing if they really want the product (because your value proposition is so good).

So, how can you easily improve the checkout process?

Here's some things to look at, but they may be disappointing for those of you looking for a quick fix or a one-size-fits-all solution . . .

DIFFERENT CHECKOUTS WORK ON DIFFERENT PLATFORMS AND DIFFERENT BUYERS

Finding the right checkout for your website requires a bit of testing. Certain checkouts work differently for certain platforms and certain buyers. For instance, we decided to do a test with a checkout that let users play with the quantity throughout the entire checkout process, up to the final stage. At any point, they could decide they wanted three of the product instead of just one. When we began using the checkout page on different platforms, we noticed that, on the iPad, the conversion rate dramatically increased. On the desktop, however, it made no difference in revenue at all.

Maybe it's psychological and iPad shoppers are in shopping mode instead of work mode, so they are more likely to increase their purchase amount. We haven't quite figured out why, but the point here is to go ahead and make small changes as long as you are tracking the results.

Different Checkouts For Different Platforms

- E.g. a checkout split test increase revenue hugely on Ipad's but not on desktop. Thus use different checkouts for different segments (N.B this test gave an extra £100k + revenue in 26 days on ipads!)

We have also tested different types of platforms and found that some are more likely to be used by those making rational purchases, while others are better for emotional buys.

Checkout

The one-page checkout on the left in the above chart worked better on sites where rational purchases were made. It also appealed to younger buyers. The one on the right is a more methodical, step-by-step approach that the older generation and those making emotional, spontaneous purchases enjoy.

The extensions for e-commerce checkout pages are simple to work with, and most often, if you've taken the time to invest in the add-to-basket rate and basket to checkout, you won't have to worry much about the final checkout-to-order confirmation step.

The secret to scaling your business is to figure out where you're losing customers.

Here's a checkout to go through to help raise the basket-to-order rate, i.e. what if it's below 30%? If you have 4000 people add something to the basket and less than 1200 proceed to checkout, then that's bad.

Let's look at the things that many people get wrong.

- Proceed to checkout below the fold. Even if people have a lot in their basket, don't let the Proceed to Checkout button get pushed down below the fold. Ideally have it both at the top and the bottom.

- Payment icons such as Visa, Mastercard, etc. These companies spend millions if not billions a year associating these logos with trust in the minds of the consumer. So, make sure you leverage this by showing them above the fold.

- Payment icons on every line item in the basket. I have seen split tests convert higher when payment icons are shown next to each item in the basket rather than just at the bottom.

- Use wording like 'continue securely' rather than 'proceed to checkout.' This split tested higher for us as people are worried about security online.

- Make sure that the basket is nicely laid out and does not look complicated. Remember perceived ease of use is pretty much equal to actual ease of use. Don't over complicate and get a usability designer to design your basket.

- Don't make your product images too small. People need to maintain the desire for the product they are buying and making them too small means they might lose their interest. The desire for the product must be bigger than the pain of paying for them.

- Have a clear colour for the Proceed to Checkout button. Make this a colour that is not used anywhere else in the design, so it stands out. Also, it should be the same colour as all the Move Forward buttons on the store, i.e. the add-to-basket, proceed-to-checkout and Confirm Order buttons should all be the same colour.

- Delivery should be clearly displayed—how long it will take and how much it will be. Preferably delivery will be free or free over a certain amount. If they have qualified for free delivery, shout about it and make it dynamic when the threshold is reached.
- If you have a free delivery threshold and the person has not hit that level yet, tell them exactly how much more they need to spend to hit free delivery, i.e. spend £5.50 more to qualify for free delivery.
- Make your return policy clear. People will be asking, what if I don't like it? Don't hide your return policy in the footer of the site. The return policy should be a good policy and it should be a selling point.
- If people use a lot of coupons on your store, make sure you monitor coupons that fail to trigger a discount. Get these to be emailed to you so you can spot common misspelling or typos of active coupons. Often you can create coupons of these typos so that you get the orders.
- Make live chat prominent on the basket page so that buyer questions can be answered quickly.
- Use countdown timers to show how long it is till they qualify for next-day delivery.
- Use countdown timers to show how long it is till the coupon they have used expires.
- Use third-party review stars and reviews to give people confidence that you can deliver the product on time.

HOW FAST ARE BUYERS ON YOUR CHECKOUT?

How do we know if the checkout is a problem?

Mark's son did swimming sports recently. He was doing well until, whilst doing backstroke, he cruised at the end because he was afraid of hitting his head on the wall. He only races once a year and he really isn't bothered about where he places.

But it made Mark think about how we had no idea if he was a fast swimmer or not. He swims a lot and seems fast, but it is only when he swims next to others do we find out if he is fast. Also, it clearly identifies an issue with his technique. Swimming at the end with one arm above your head for a quarter length of the pool, just in case you hit your head, is going to slow you down a bit. Now we know what's wrong we can fix it.

This is like your checkout page.

It looks fine.

Chugging all day and sending you order confirmation emails.

But how fast is it?

Let's have a look at five retailers and see how long people on average spend on the checkout page. After this we can compare the results.

Some of our clients use the one-step checkout, which is all the checkout on one page and thus makes it easy to find the 'time on page' for each one. Here's how they looked last month:

- B2B Site A selling spare parts: Average time on checkout page—3 minutes 7 seconds.
- B2B Site B selling lab equipment: Average time on checkout page—3 minutes 40 seconds.
- B2C Site C selling clothing: Average time on checkout page—2 minutes 50 seconds.
- B2B Site D selling protective equipment: Average time on checkout page—2 minutes 33 seconds.
- B2C Site E selling food: Average time on checkout page—2 minutes 32 seconds.
- B2C Site F selling flowers: Average time on checkout page—3 minutes 59 seconds.

So how does the checkout race look?

Well, we might argue that Business 2 Business (B2B) site checkouts are a little slower than Business to Consumer (B2C) sites. This would make sense as people might have to look up addresses, etc., when buying for work.

But site F selling flowers does look slow, doesn't it? Almost 4 minutes against an average time on B2B sites of 2–3 minutes.

Next step would be to record some browser sessions of site E and then some browser sessions of site F.

We could then compare the behaviour and find out what people are struggling with.

Where there is struggle, there is always checkout abandonment, so this will be very lucrative work indeed.

THINK ABOUT THE FLOW OF BUYER

Next we want to introduce the concept of 'visitor flow' through the website. Don't treat each page on your site as an island, just as important is how people move through those pages.

A good metaphor for an e-commerce customer journey is packing to go on holiday.

When Mark travels he likes to pack well in advance and check he has everything he might need. Contact lens solution, swimming trunks, glasses—all the things he has forgotten in the past. He packs and then checks his suitcase a lot to make sure it's still correct.

He always checks that he has his passport multiple times before he leaves the house, even though he knows it's there. He has multiple items to pack and he wants to be confident that he has them.

His nervousness around packing is exactly how buyers feel about their basket on an e-commerce site.

Most e-commerce stores seem to think that there is a one-size-fits-all strategy to how the flow should work on their websites.

By flow we mean what happens when someone adds something to their basket, where they get taken and what happens.

They go and see how Amazon does it or ASOS and then copy that.

Many sites keep people on the product page and then have a 'hover reveal' for the basket icon to show what's in the basket. If people want to actually visit the basket page, then they have to click in the basket reveal to see basket.

Often some of these sites funnel people directly to the checkout.

Nobody seems to question this.

But the flow people take when moving through the site has a massive impact on the conversion rate.

There is no one size fits all.

Why is this?

Because on some sites people tend to only add one item to the basket and check out (a dress website). Other sites, like a herb and spices site, people will tend to add five to seven items to the basket before checking out.

On sites that people add more items to the basket on average, the basket is an important page.

Coming back to our packing analogy. If we were packing a suitcase and could not look in the suitcase once we'd put something in it, then we would get nervous when leaving the house.

How could we check we had everything we needed?

This nervousness increases with the number of items people add to the basket. We need to reduce this nervousness to a minimum if we want people to check out. On many sites with many items in the basket, the basket hover in the top right just doesn't cut it.

The customer is not aware of why they are nervous, they can see what's in the basket on the hover. But because the hover is small and hard to see it does not give them the confidence that seeing the products nicely laid out on the basket page does.

When we worked on the conversion rate for one of the world's largest wine sites we told them that people needed to be taken to the basket page when they added something to the basket. This simple change gave them an extra 3 million GBP in revenue per year. This was because the wine site made people order a crate of wine and choose at least six bottles. They needed to be on the basket page to see the collection they had chosen and fall in love with it. They couldn't engage with the wines they had chosen on a small hover window.

If you have a high average amount of different products in customers' baskets, don't skip the basket page. It's important.

You need to map out the flow of your site to fit how your shoppers shop. Don't blindly copy other websites; even your competitors have probably got it wrong.

The flow of the purchase is key.

HOW TO RAISE THIS KPI—BASKET TO ORDER RATE

Here are some quick wins for you from our time in the trenches.

- Make sure you use a tool like Mouseflow to capture users' sessions on the checkout pages. We built a team in the Philippines just to do this as we found lots and lots of errors and quick fixes on basically any site we looked at. Mouseflow has a good tag called 'click rage' which shows when people get really frustrated and this can lead to areas where there are problems.

- Look for JavaScript errors in Mouseflow recordings as it can highlight a particular platform, e.g. Amazon Silk, that does not work with your website. Often these are easy fixes.
- The basket page also needs to sell; don't have a tick-in-the-box basket page, it needs to drive momentum throughout the sale. Make sure the basket page answers all the objections people have at this stage such as:
  » How much is delivery?
  » What about returns?
  » Is this item difficult to deliver?
  » How much discount am I getting?
  » How quick is delivery?
  » What guarantees is there about this product?
  » Why should we do this today rather than tomorrow?
- Also, don't think that one checkout flow is going to work across all devices. What works on desktop might totally annoy on the mobile site. Split test each platform separately and find what works for each. Mobile is much more about ease of use; desktop is more about convincability.
- Is your lost password functionality annoying? If they have just typed in their email and got the wrong password, then for god's sake, remember the email just typed in on the lost password form. Such a silly, easy thing to do but hardly anyone does it.
- For people who cannot remember their password let them check out as guests if they want and just add their order to the same email address if it exists in the database. Make it easy, not hard.
- Make reward points easy to understand, easy to add, paint-by-numbers approach rather than *War and Peace.*
- Keep a picture of the products all the way through the checkout, especially if you are selling aspirational items. Taking the product imagery away will separate the user from the want of the item, making it easier for them to abandon.
- Add social proof all the way through the checkout: David just bought, etc.

- Use secure wording on the checkout to show that the checkout is secure and not likely to get hacked.
- Bring payment logos like Visa, Mastercard above the fold and add them to each line item on the basket. These billion-dollar firms spend untold millions each year associating these brand logos with trust. Leverage their marketing spend to increase checkout conversion rates.
- Split test Checkout and Basket Proceed button colours; it can have more impact than you would expect.
- Split test removing the main navigation for the checkout pages. Do people get distracted and leave the site for Facebook, etc.?
- Split test using one-click ordering services like Amazon Pay, Paypal Express, etc., to see if this increases conversion.
- For B2B sites offer an invoice option.
- Offer an AfterPay-type payment service where the user can split the payment into 10 payments, interest free.
- Add live chat to the checkout page that listens for page activity that could signal issues, such as javascript errors, click rage, the filling out of fields over and over, or the repeated clicking of buttons. Then auto prompt, 'Are you having an issue we can help with?.' Make this help 24/7 by using UK and overseas teams for this important page. At the very least the chat support team can raise a ticket and make sure it does not happen again.

RECAP: BASKET-TO-ORDER RATE

The issues that prevent customers from getting from the basket to checkout are typically small, yet significant. Trouble with coupons or the use of PayPal Express are two of the most common problems we see.

KPI: BASKET-TO-ORDER RATE

The number of orders divided by the people that add an item to the basket.

Put it to use:

- Only 55% of people who add something to their basket will proceed to checkout.
- Simple things can result in lost customers, such as coupon codes with one digit wrong.
- PayPal Express works well with new customers, but not with recurring customers. New customers don't trust you yet.
- Display every detail, including cost of product, delivery options and payment icons on the basket page. There should be no surprises.
- 84% of customers go from the checkout to order confirmation.
- Split test different types of checkouts on different platforms to see what works best.

Answer the following:

- Do you offer coupon codes? If so, what happens, right now, if a customer enters the coupon code wrong? How would you handle it better? Think of it the same way a physical sales assistant would.
- Split test your checkout payment options. See which one works better: Paypal Express or credit card payments. Which one is more successful on your website?
- What does your checkout basket look like? Are all the details a customer needs in one place? Write down where the basket is excelling and where it is lacking.
- Does your checkout work on all platforms? Check this carefully. If your checkout isn't working on an iPad, but works on the desktop, you could be losing customers.

*See back of book for all of our recaps and step-by-step instructions for KPIs all in one handy workbook.

KPI SUCCESS DEPENDS ON YOU

Are we making e-commerce too complicated?

Often when we brainstorm about a new customer and how to grow their revenue, we imagine the online store as a physical store. This visualisation makes everything seem much simpler.

Just imagine you are a supermarket manager.

You come into work and an employee tells you that 100 people have abandoned their shopping trolleys full of food. The obvious question would be, where did they do this and why? Let's say that they all abandoned at the fish counter because of the smell. Well, you can fix that.

However, on an online store, unless you have set up Google Analytics add-to-basket events, it's impossible to know where those full baskets are being left.

Creating a segment in Google Analytics to only show people who add something to the basket and then exit the site without buying is fascinating. What tends to emerge is some category pages where people just give up and knowing this means you can optimise these pages.

Coming back to the supermarket analogy, imagine walking past the self-checkouts and seeing customers kicking the tills in frustration. Again, you would do something about it, yet on a website click rage is common and most of the time not seen and not acted upon.

If 25 people asked your supermarket employees a question, like 'Where is the Gouda cheese?' and got an answer and then you watched the customers run out the door, you would know something was wrong. Onsite search has exits like this every day.

Or how about people walking a supermarket aisle with only one item in their basket, ignoring everything else. Not one person, but many people. As a supermarket boss you would talk to them and ask why they don't buy something else at the same time. You would get instant feedback, but it's not common to survey customers on an e-commerce store and make changes.

The point is that what's not seen gets ignored. You need to bring the pain of your customers right smack bang in front of your team, so it gets acted upon. It's hard to watch customers leave the store. Buy a big TV and show live users on the store moving their cursor, so that everyone understands what's important.

WHERE TO START

A good e-commerce owner is like a great investor. The main decision is where to invest time and money.

Joel Greenblatt's book *You Can Be a Stock Market Genius* sounds like a lofty title. But when you look at Joel Greenblatt's investing track record you must take your hat off to him. Over a 10-year period he averaged a 50% return on investment.

That's crazy good! This means that every 1.7 years he would have doubled your money.

So, what's his secret?

Well, there are many investments you can make but you don't have to make them all. Joel focuses on those investment areas where he has the wind behind him.

He looks for special situations where in the past on average things have gone well.

Take spinoffs, for example; on average, these tend to outperform the market. So if you invest in spinoffs, you are already playing off the 'ladies tee' and starting a little ahead of the market.

He also invests in areas that are too complicated for the average investor to understand or are places that stink and put investors off. If he can find an area where most people will put it into the 'too hard' basket but with a bit of digging gold nuggets can be found, this is where he will invest. Here he would look for bankruptcies, warrants and options.

Again, because a lot of the competition has given up the wind is behind him when he makes an investment based on sound research.

So, what's this got to do with us as e-commerce site owners?

Well, we are investing in our websites all the time, either in time or in actual money. Where we allocate that spend is important is it dictates the return we get. Also given it's our own business we should be getting decent returns.

If we are to invest in our businesses like Joel, then we must look for where the wind is behind us. This means looking for what's already working and making this go further. Don't invest in everything, invest more in what's working. Invest in the product categories that do well. Invest in the customer types that buy the most. Invest in the marketing channels that work.

This might sound obvious.

But time after time we see e-commerce sites trying to expand to new countries before they have maxed out the marketing spend in their own market. We see sites adding new product ranges when they have not dominated the existing categories they serve.

We must also look for those 'too hard' categories that other competitors avoid but customers want. Think back 10 years in e-commerce and those businesses that first offered 'free delivery, free returns.' Much of the competition would have put this into the 'too hard' category thinking that they would lose money. But those that tried it realised it was a winner.

If you are a business to business site, maybe customers want a certain payment plan or buying on account. Most sites will put this down as 'too hard' but it might be a game changer.

WHERE TO END

Where to end? This is a trick question because there really is no end to the optimisations you can do.

In this book we have been looking at the KPIs and sales funnels as a whole across all marketing channels and traffic types. But as you grow you can segment them down into silos that make sense, such as AdWords, existing customers, new customers, lapsed, etc.

Doing this fits nicely into the wave of artificial intelligence that's being applied to e-commerce as we write.

It's the dawn of AI and that's here to stay for e-commerce.

What this means for us marketers is that the one-size-fits-all split test just does not cut it anymore.

Look at the tests run over the past five years on sites like WhichTestWon and you will see big AB split tests mostly across all traffic; for example, split testing two different category header images is now dead. We need to go deeper.

How?

With artificial intelligence adding to the equation we need to think of our e-commerce site as not one site, but many sites for all the segments of users coming to it.

Given that, for now at least, the magic number of conversions per month needed for an AI engine to optimise on Facebook and AdWords seems to be around 50, we need to slice the website into at least 50 conversions a month.

This might look like the following segments:

- Existing customers who bought within the last six months.
- Existing customers who bought within the last 12 months.
- New visitors.
- Repeat visitors within the past 30 days but never bought.
- Lapsed customers.

If we have at least 50 conversions per month for each of these segments, then we should be able to optimise them further.

Once you are done, you might have very different user experiences for each segment, as what converts one segment might lower the conversion rate in one and vice versa.

Using free tools like Google Optimize we can start to segment the traffic into silos like the above and find out exactly what makes them buy.

You will find out that the traffic to your site is very different in motivation and buying trigger. For example, we found that for segment 1, making the reward points on the checkout MASSIVE had a big difference in their conversion rate. However, reducing the reward points prominence for segment 3 had no effect and instead putting in testimonials here was much better.

The key eyeball real estate on your e-commerce store is quite small. The places that people focus on are narrow and they will miss your main sales points unless positioned carefully. For example, an existing customer knows you have free returns and free delivery and so might respond better to other messaging, whereas this is key for first-time buyers.

So, start cutting your traffic into segment silos and throw some variants at an AI engine and let it find out what converts best.

It's exciting times.

IN SUMMARY

Lastly, remember that your KPI success ultimately depends on you.

Let's recap the most important points. You'll need to define your KPIs and use

Google Analytics and other methods to determine whether your site falls below the average statistics in the three areas we've established:

✓   11% of visitors will add a product to their basket.

✓   Of that 11%, 55% will proceed to checkout.

✓   Of that 55%, 84% will place an order.

The other KPIs are going to be unique to your industry and so it's important to measure them and improve them. While this book is a start, it's hard to provide different industries with a blanket rule of thumb. You need a professional to look at the statistics and evaluate the ins and outs of your website for the best results.

Start with the bounce rate for your categories, products and search results at the add-to-basket, basket-to-checkout and check-to-order confirmation steps, then invest your time and money at the most critical point.

Once you've finished this, benchmark your website against your defined KPIs again. Repeat the process, month after month, to ensure your e-commerce site continues to perform the way you want it to and provides you with the increased revenue you're looking for.

Most importantly, don't rely on your e-commerce agency to do everything for you. Get into the mix and evaluate your category pages, product pages and search terms yourself. Many of these items may not work the way you want them to, but you may have better insight into the reason why. You know your product better than anyone—or you should!

After you have this down, create longer-term KPIs and goals, such as:

Longer term KPIs must be set e.g. :

• Conversion Rate 3% average
• Traffic 350000 average per month
• PPC Cost per conversion - average under £15
• AOV - £55
• Add to basket percentage - 18%
• Proceed to Checkout percentage - 55%
• Checkout to Order percentage - 50%
• Repeat Order Per Year Average - 2 times a year

Also, set KPI targets for add to basket, basket to order, AOV, traffic, etc., to take into seasonality. Some months you're naturally going to want to spend more on AdWords and reach for higher conversion rates. This is one of the first things we do with our new clients. We get the monthly KPIs sorted out so that we know how well we are doing each month.

Continually come back and decide where you want to invest to keep on increasing your statistics. This will result in steady and predictable scaling of your e-commerce business, and that's exactly what you want!

We hope this information has helped bring clarity to the way you think about your products and the entire purchasing process on your e-commerce site.

Keep learning and growing!

We are always here to help.

GO FOR IT

Recently we had lunch with a good friend of ours.

He runs a very successful e-commerce store selling outdoor sports goods.

He started with about 5K worth of personal funds and has grown in five years to be a global business turning over millions.

We dropped what we thought was a simple question.

'If you went back three years what changes would you make to your business knowing what you know now?'

He replied, 'I would set my expectations higher; the only reason we didn't do more revenue that year was because I thought that it was a big number. If I had changed my outlook and believed that x turnover was too low, then we would have done more.'

We see this a lot.

Sometimes the limit on an e-commerce business is our own belief in what it can do. We think that hitting a million in sales is amazing because we have never hit it before. But what if you could easily be doing more?

Have you set your business thermostat too low?

Why have you set it at that level?

Could it go much higher?

If you spend 5K on AdWords and get back 40K—why not spend more?

We don't realise how scarce the opportunity is or how time dependent it is;

even more so if this is our first e-commerce business and it's a big hit. Imagine you are prospecting for gold and you hit it big first dig. You would be convinced you were a gold mining genius. However, if you have been digging for gold for years and failed and failed, when you hit gold you would realise how difficult it is.

If you have good arbitrage in your business, let it run, as it's as rare as hen's teeth and there are a thousand people behind you trying to find the vein of gold you are sitting on.

Go for it, now, today!

KPI WORKBOOK

KPI 1: ADD-TO-BASKET RATE

Your product pages are just as, if not more, important than your category pages, especially when using Google Shopping. Make sure all essential details and the Add to Basket button is above the fold, provide info about other similar items and make sure customers can easily return to previous products they were looking at.

KPI: ADD-TO-BASKET RATE

Put it to use:
- 11% of visitors should be adding to their baskets. If your percentage is less than 11%, this KPI needs attention.
- Determine your type of buyer: spontaneous, methodical, humanistic or competitive.
- Adjust your product pages so that all pertinent information occurs above the fold. This makes it easier for customers to see everything and make quick decisions.
- Look at the middle reviews to determine what your site is doing wrong.
- Improve your worst-performing searches to increase add-to-basket rate.

Answer the following questions:
- What type of buyer does your website appeal to? Why?

- Take a look at your product pages and category pages. What areas can you improve on?

- What is your worst-performing search? Why do you think it performs so poorly?

- Take a look at your middle reviews. What areas do these reviews indicate need work? Write out your plan for improvement here.

KPI 2: WEBSITE SPEED AND CAPACITY

Customers spend an average of six minutes on your website. If your site is running slow, they'll achieve a lot less in that amount of time than if it is running at a high speed. The faster your website speed, the higher your average order value and conversion rate will be.

KPI: WEBSITE SPEED AND CAPACITY

Put it to use:
- Slow page load can cause Google penalties that affect your page ranking.
- Measure your web speed often. This will help increase conversion rates.
- Google Analytics can help you measure your website speed, as well as other sites like www.webpagetest.org.
- Your site should measure under four seconds.
- Increasing speed and capacity involves using clean code, varnish caching and optimising the server.

Answer the following questions:
- Have you experienced slow page load recently or seen a lot of browser abandonment from visitors?

- What is your current website speed? Use the information in this chapter to check the speed via webpagetest.org and Google Analytics.

- What are three things that could be causing the reduction in website speed? How can you fix them?

- Are there certain times of the year when you need more website capacity (e.g. Black Friday, Christmas)?

- How do you plan on making sure your website is ready for visitors during this peak time?

KPI 3: LIFETIME CUSTOMER VALUE

Tracking lifetime customer value involves a number of different steps, including considering the type of customers you have, the coupons they use, their overall satisfaction and their delivery choices.

KPI: LIFETIME CUSTOMER VALUE—THE TOTAL REVENUE DIVIDED BY THE TOTAL NUMBER OF CUSTOMERS.

Put it to use:
- LTCV helps you track the products that lead to the highest lifetime value.
- Providing discount coupons, in the right setting, helps increase lifetime value.
- Use ScentTrail to track the type of customers you recruit and which products work best to recruit them.
- Upload customer email lists in Google AdWords so you can continually show your ad or products to customers on the list.
- Track this KPI regularly and watch it year after year to see how it changes.

Answer the following questions:
- What customers are you recruiting? Does your business naturally lead to high repeat purchase rates?

- What delivery options do your customers choose most often? What delivery rates do repeat customers opt for?

- Has your average review rating increased or decreased since your business began? This can tell you immediately whether your customers are happy with you and your products.

- How do you track the effect of marketing channels? After reading this chapter, what do you think the benefits of using ScentTrail to track LTCV marketing channels would be?

- Would you be willing to offer a lapsed customer a special rate if it meant increasing your LTCV overall? What type of special offer do you think would encourage a lapsed customer to come back to your website and make a purchase?

KPI 4: GROWTH OF SIX-MONTH CUSTOMER RECRUITMENT YEAR ON YEAR

Your recruitment rate should stay the same or increase year on year. If you compare the last six months to the same time last year and the rate is lower, there is a definite issue. Sometimes it's another KPI. Other KPIs that affect conversion rates can affect your recruitment rate. Fixing these other indicators will usually help increase this KPI.

KPI: GROWTH OF SIX-MONTH CUSTOMER RECRUITMENT YEAR ON YEAR

This refers to the total number of customers you have recruited in the last six months. Add these together, then compare them to the same data gathered the prior year.

Put it to use:
- This KPI helps you determine if your business will continue to grow.
- Cannot be found in Google Analytics, but may be worked out in Excel.
- If this number declines, it means you're experiencing less growth. This is a warning sign.
- Some KPIs will affect your recruitment rate. If they aren't doing well, your recruitment rate will show it.

Answer the following questions:
- Use an Excel sheet to calculate your current six-month recruitment rate. What is it? Compare it to the previous year's. Did the amount increase, decrease or stay the same?

- If the number decreased, look at the other KPIs. Are they functioning as they should be? If not, what steps will you take to resolve this issue?

- Consider other trackable things you've done to contribute to a lower recruitment number. Write them here and check each one.

- What marketing channels do you use? How are they performing?

- What steps can you take next to increase your six-month customer recruitment rate year on year?

KPI 5: AVERAGE ORDER VALUE ROBUSTNESS

While perhaps not the first KPI you look at, the average order value is probably the most important of all seven. If this value is too low, your add-to-basket rate or checkout-to-order rate cannot grow. It also affects your lifetime customer value, revenue and marketing costs.

KPI: AVERAGE ORDER VALUE ROBUSTNESS

The average, compared year on year, of the average value of orders and traffic growth.

Put it to use:

- You should always keep an eye on your average order value, as it can stifle or improve growth, depending on whether it is low or high.
- You should have a high AOV and 1.5x purchase frequency per year or a low AOV and 5x purchase frequency per year.
- As you increase the amount of traffic and the conversion rate of your website, your AOV should increase as well.
- If your AOV isn't robust enough, it can negatively affect other KPIs.
- Increasing the customer's basket size or checkout amount can improve AOV.

Answer the following questions:

- What is your average order value? It is high or low compared to the traffic rate and conversion rate you have?

- What are three products on your website that are frequently purchased together?

- What are three ways you can increase your average order value?

- Do you normally offer bundles? Do you think your customers would be open to purchasing more from you if they got a bundled promotion at a slight discount? Why or why not?

KPI 6: TRAFFIC GROWTH

To increase the amount of traffic to your online store, you need to be able to pay more for a customer than your competitor can. This means making sure all of your KPIs, especially lifetime customer value and add to basket, are improved so your traffic resources are available and you are able to increase your traffic numbers.

KPI: TRAFFIC GROWTH

Put it to use:
- Increase traffic with SEO. With a great marketing strategy and e-commerce structural SEO, you can achieve natural traffic through Google.
- Make sure the e-commerce structure is correct or it can lead to bad SEO.
- The way your website operates affects revenue and traffic growth. Slow sites kill traffic.
- Use Google Page Speed or YSlow for page speed times. Google Analytics tends to get confused.

Answer the following questions:
- How well are your other KPIs performing? Can you afford to move your attention to this KPI or do you need to spend more time on the add-to-basket KPI or LTCV KPI first?

- Is your e-commerce implemented correctly? If you can't answer this question, or you can't say yes for certain, get the help of a professional. A poor structure leads to poor results.

- How often do you test the speed of your website? What speed tests do you use? What is your average load time?

KPI 7: BASKET-TO-ORDER RATE

The issues that prevent customers from getting from the basket to checkout are typically small, yet significant. Trouble with coupons or the use of PayPal Express are two of the most common problems we see.

KPI: BASKET-TO-ORDER RATE

The number of orders divided by the people that add an item to the basket.

Put it to use:
- Only 55% of people who add something to their basket will proceed to checkout.
- Simple things can result in lost customers, such as coupon codes with one digit wrong.
- PayPal Express works well with new customers, but not with recurring customers. New customers don't trust you yet.
- Display every detail, including cost of product, delivery options and payment icons on the basket page. There should be no surprises.
- 84% of customers go from the checkout to order confirmation.
- Split test different types of checkouts on different platforms to see what works best.

Answer the following questions:
- Do you offer coupon codes? If so, what happens, right now, if a customer enters the coupon code wrong? How would you handle it better? Think of it the same way a physical sales assistant would.

- Split test your checkout payment options. See which one work better: Paypal Express or credit card payments. Which one is more successful on your website?

- What does your checkout basket look like? Are all the details a customer needs in one place? Write down where the basket is excelling and where it is lacking.

- Does your checkout work on all platforms? Check this carefully. If your checkout isn't working on an iPad, but works on the desktop, you could be losing customers.

APPENDIX

APPENDIX

THE 12 COMMANDMENTS OF E-COMMERCE

Why 12?

No idea. 10 would be biblical and 20 would be too much.

Here you go.

1. Create a KPI plan for each month. Make sure you have targets for average order value, traffic, add-to-basket % and basket-to-order % each month. Otherwise, how will you know how you went?

2. Things change. Embrace them. Marketing is moving faster than ever. Don't hold on to things that used to work but no longer get results.

3. Have a beginner's mind. The day you stop learning is the day you stop growing. Never think you are the best; there are always people to learn from.

4. If you're scared of investing in site and growth, e-commerce isn't for you. Sell or get a job.

5. Be brave enough to make offers that seem outrageous to the competition; if they work, no one will copy them for a long time.

6. Design your site for one person; make it personal to that main buyer persona.

7. You can't sell the same product that others sell more cheaply unless you are famous or the Mafia.

8. Don't do marketing that you cannot track the results of.

9. Build good arbitrage that you can leverage. Lower cost back office, lower cost delivery, famous products, exclusive product, reward points. You need something to arbitrage off.

10. Have min and max marketing budgets per month. Spend more when return is good and less when it's not. Don't try and spend the same each month. Make hay when the sun shines.

11. Competitors are mostly idiots, don't copy them blindly. Seek out the few that get it.

12. Be creative artists on the shop front but like a military operation in the warehouse.